MOVIN' ON UP

A Woman's Guide Beyond Religion To Spirit Living

Rebecca Fl  ovo

Dabar Publishing Company

P.O. Box 35377 · Detroit, MI 48235

Unless otherwise noted, all Scripture quotations are from the King James Version of the Bible.

Scripture quotations marked (NIV) are taken from the Holy Bible, New International Version ® Copyright © 1973, 1978, 1984 by International Bible Society. Used by permission of Zondervan Publishing House. All rights reserved.

Publisher's Cataloging in Publication
Osaigbovo, Rebecca.
    Movin' On Up: A Woman's Guide Beyond Religion to Spirit Living/Rebecca Osaigbovo.—1st ed.
      p. cm.
    Includes bibliographical references
ISBN 1-880560-55-0 (cloth).—ISBN 1-880560-54-2 (pbk.)
      1. African American Women-Religious Life-Christian Theology 1. Title
  E185.86 1992 / 301.242/ Church Library:258.843
Library of Congress Catalog Card Number 97-065147

PRINTED IN THE UNITED STATES OF AMERICA

Dedication

This book is dedicated to the memory
of two special women who literally
have moved on up.

My mother: Shermine Florence
and my sister: Beverly Cox.

I speak the breath of God to
the vast army of handmaidens
whom God has called to take their place
so that the Body of Christ
can go to another level in the Spirit.
May God's Spirit move you on up;
May God's Spirit move you on through;
May God's Spirit be your life.

Acknowledgments

I appreciate the many pastors who have welcomed me into their churches to teach their women over the past several years. I also appreciate the many women who, after listening to me, have encouraged me.

My husband, Uwaifo's (pronounced *Why-fo*) help has been invaluable. He has read the manuscript at different stages and has given excellent direction. My children, Esosa, Esohe, Nosa Osaigbovo, and Ethan Cox have all helped out in different ways: typing, relieving me of other duties, hugs, and understanding.

I thank Vanessa Boyden, Joy Gaddis, Victoria Johnson, Denise Spence, and Brenda Watkins for their listening ear and encouragement in conversations that have helped me solidify concepts in this book. They have also provided valuable critique.

Appreciation for editorial help goes to Clarinda Gipson, Elaine Rottman, and Diane Reeder. I thank Maureen LeLaucher and Sheri Lee for proofreading assistance and my brother, William Florence for typesetting assistance. Others who have had a part to play in this book, giving very helpful feedback are: Andrell Sturdivant, Jannie Wilcoxson, Barbara Shealey, Frances Moore, Arthur Jackson, Gregory Alexander, Helen Harris and Sybil Fraiser.

I am grateful to the artistic skills of Lynette Gibson, who gets credit for the front cover design and most of the art work throughout this book. Todd Dixson is responsible for the illustrations in Chapter 14. I also appreciate John Watkins' contribution of labor and skills to the cover design. Credit goes to AM Photography Studio of Detroit, Michigan for the photographs on the cover.

I want to acknowledge the hundreds of ministers God has used in my life to equip me. I have read their books and listened to their tapes, teachings, and sermons. Though it would be impossible for me to name each man or woman God has used, God knows.

Most of all, I praise God for His abundant grace and mercy; and His love and faithfulness to me. He, alone should receive full credit for any help anyone receives from this book.

TABLE OF CONTENTS

Foreword

Rebecca Osaigbovo has done it again. This latest book, *Moving On Up*, is as profound as its predecessor, *Chosen Vessels*.

In Chosen Vessels, Rebecca told African American women that it is imperative they be involved in the process of bringing about change in our communities.

Moving On Up goes deeper, showing women in the Body of Christ how God wants to live through them. Rebecca spares no punches, digging deep into proper attitudes of the heart, not just of outward actions. She shows how even women in the most vital ministries can be sidetracked—even deceived—into dependence on their own strength rather than God's control. This book allows the reader to go with Rebecca as she candidly shares her personal journey on the path to Spirit-filled living.

Rebecca does not remove herself from ordinary people as though she possesses some secret knowledge or has the authority to give out rules that should work in theory. Neither does she make God's holy relationship and ministry in our lives commonplace or trite. If we believe that God has called women to live transcendent lives, it will be difficult to deny the spiritual truths and applications found in this book.

Though *Moving On Up* is written primarily to women, I believe that its application goes beyond gender and can be an inspiration to men, as well. Many of God's children will be encouraged by these words, and gain insight that they can apply in practical ways in their daily lives. Those of us who have chosen to walk with God in loving obedience will find this book a welcome breath of fresh air. I highly recommend *Moving On Up*, and thank God for raising up a woman like Rebecca to provide this timely and much needed message of encouragement.

Dr. John M. Perkins
John M. Perkins Foundation for Reconciliation and Development

SECTION I

Prerequisite to Spirit Living

CHAPTER 1

The Journey

"Remember ye not the former things, neither consider the things of old. Behold I will do a new thing; now it shall spring forth."

Isaiah 43:18, 19

I HAVE BEEN VERY EXCITED to see what God is doing in the lives of women around this country as I have been privileged to meet some of God's chosen vessels. Women in Cleveland and L.A. are talking about joining together to take back their communities. Women in New Orleans are meeting together and really sharing their struggles at a deep level that I have seldom seen. The women in Moncks Corner, South Carolina have been praying for years and have seen what God can do in their midst. From Boston to San Jose, African American women are waking up. Everywhere I go, women are hungry for God. They want truth. Some of the things I teach in my seminars, as in this book, are not easy to swallow, but I have experienced a receptivity to the Word of God that I did not believe would be there. I am grateful to God. From what I've seen, I believe that many Christian women really do want to move beyond religion to Spirit living.

The journey to unconditional love

The bottom line is love. Love is the command God has given us. Love is what identifies us as Christians. Love is the key to Spirit living and maturity. Everything God does in our lives is designed to cause us to love Him with all of our hearts and to help us relate to others by operating in His kind of love.

The task at hand for all of us is that we might love with unconditional love in fuller, deeper, more creative ways. The task is that we must forgive more freely, more quickly, and in greater measure than we ever have before. The capacity to care and forgive must get wider, deeper, and broader as we continue to walk this love walk.

Loving God first with all of our heart, soul, mind, and strength seems to be such a far-fetched reality for many. Yet Jesus Christ, the Son of God himself, told us to do this as the first commandment. I happen to believe that obeying the first commandment, along with the second commandment to love our neighbors as ourselves, is the key to peace, security, health, provision for us as individuals, and for the Body of Christ as a whole, and the only hope for change in a world laden with evil, unrest and darkness.

In this book, I will attempt to identify the various parts of the journey I took to get to be wholly God's: loving Him with all of my heart, soul, mind, and strength. I will also take you along on my journey to learn to love and serve others with God's unconditional love. Perhaps my story will help you understand what God is doing in your life. Your journey of unconditional love will not be identical to mine. Yours will reflect your specific circumstances, history, and personality.

The Way is Jesus! Come with me as we explore Him. I invite you to get caught up, tangled up, and tied up in Jesus in ways you have not experienced before. There is more that God wants to do in you and through you. Please don't settle for less than the very best. Avoid the temptation to rest in spots along the way. Yes, we do have a rest awaiting with Him. But let's press on to get there, forgetting what's behind. Yes, God is working mightily in His people. But let's not settle for the "good" when the "great" is yet to come.

> Remember ye not the former things, neither consider the things of old. Behold, I will do a new thing, now it shall spring forth:

Shall ye not know it? I will even make a way in the wilderness and rivers in the desert (Isaiah 43:18, 19).

The Lord promised a new thing in the above Scripture. I believe that new thing is upon us now! It's a new day, my friends. There is just no comparison with the old. Let's not look back at the old, but let's reach for and walk in this new day.

For women

This book is for women. Some things simply are unique to women. In another book I've written, *Chosen Vessels: Women of Color, Keys to Change*, we discussed how God endorsed the adversarial relationship between Satan and women.[1] Women suffer abuse today, in large part, because the enemy does not want women to be on the offensive. He does not want them to wake up and realize that they are his enemies. Satan's objective is multifaceted. He wants to destroy a woman's purpose, rendering her powerless to affect her family, friends, and community. Ultimately, Satan wants to take her whole life.

Though this book is for all women, it does have a distinct "chocolate" flavor. It was written with the African American Christian woman in mind. I make no apologies for that. I am African American. I serve the African American community and my heart's desire is for my people. There are some things that are unique to us that I will address. By using the term "African American women," it is not my intention to exclude those who are not African American. Rather, it is my intent to say, "African American Christian woman, God esteems you highly. He knows your unique pain. He has not forgotten about you. He has chosen you." Because truth knows no color, this book will benefit any woman who cares to read it.

Women are important keys to change. As a result, they have been attacked with much pain and abuse. God desires to give His

Spirit in abundance to heal those of us who are wounded. God is big and His grace is greater than our pain or sin. The only reasonable response to His grace is to learn to live and walk in the Spirit—not to just visit, but to actually live there consistently. As more women do that, our families and communities will respond accordingly.

A guide

To write a book on spiritual maturity could be presumptuous. Does it mean that I think I'm spiritually mature? Do I consider myself an expert on spirituality? Have I arrived, so now I can tell you how to get there?

I answer a resounding "No!" to all of the above. I believe God has done a lot in my life over the 37 years I've known Him. I know I'm not where I was ten years ago. But growing up spiritually did not come the way I had expected it. I thought I was responsible for my maturity. I had little knowledge of God's grace and His ability to initiate and orchestrate our growth.

Spirituality and spiritual growth are not easily understood. This book is not written to give one, two, or three steps to spiritual growth. We don't need another formula for victorious Christian living. We like formulas because that gives us something to memorize and do. That's much easier than relating personally to a God we sometimes don't understand, and who sometimes is silent.

God's intent is for each of us to know Him in a deep intimate relationship that goes beyond keeping appointments with Him to a moment-by-moment dependence on Him as our life source. God can bring us into this level of intimacy. I believe He has as many different ways to do this as there are people on the earth. The way He took me to Himself will not be exactly the way He'll take you. I'm glad I am unique and have the Master Designer's plan for spiritual maturity. So what I share in this book are principles to help you follow the Master Designer's plan for you. That's why I call it a guide. I don't know God's exact plan for you, but from my experience, I can guide you to the place where you'll be more comfortable with where He's taking you. I have not arrived, but you can benefit from my journey thus far.

Then perhaps together we can all move on up to that position very few have attained. I think we will find that the closer we come to that place, the more we will need each other. God never intended us to be so independent in our spiritual growth or even in our pursuit of Him. It is only when we are in proper relationship with others who also want to love Him with all their hearts that we can make it.

Come, as I share with you what I've discovered. The ideas may be shocking. The conclusions may be radical. The way up and out may require unconventional measures. But I believe God will give us the means to move on up to Spirit living if we are willing to move beyond our comfort zones. My desire in writing this book is to stir up the thousands of women who have been called to come on up higher. That's not to devalue how far He has brought us; it's just to say there is another place He wants to take us.

I hope to give insight and understanding that will keep you moving on up! It's so easy to turn back. I've done it hundreds of times, many times without knowing what I was doing. Maybe you can be spared some of the frustration and waste of time.

Beyond religion

There are many roadblocks and traps as we make the journey to that place of living in the Spirit. Unfortunately, religion is one of the traps. Because Satan knows women naturally gravitate towards things that are religious, he has to find a way for us to be religious without really living in the Spirit.

This book will help you understand the difference between Spirit living and religion. As you will see, there is one religion that is a major roadblock to Spirit living. It's an understanding and application of Christianity that I believe was cooked up in hell to confuse and destroy authentic Christians. It's been perfected in the western world.

Most sincere Christians are caught up in a mixture of the real and the false. This book will guide you out of the false way, if you are willing to make the sacrifice. It will not be easy, but it will be worth it. It is also necessary if you want to be a woman to whom Jesus will say, "Well done, my good and faithful servant."

To Spirit living

There is a place in God, a place of the Spirit in which we can dwell, a secret place of the Most High, under the shadow of the Almighty (Psalm 91:3). It's a place where all the promises of God are ours. It's a place where we overcome the world, the flesh, and the Devil. It's a place we often talk and hear about, but very few ever make it there. It's the place where the Devil can't touch us. It's a place where God can use us to destroy the works of the Devil.

Women have a key place in what God is doing today. This book will discuss how women *must* come to a place of spiritual maturity by consistently living in the Spirit in order to fulfill their destiny in God.

The goal is to help you live in the power of the Spirit. Because many women are involved in religious activity, they fail to tap the tremendous amount of spiritual power available to them. This is why we can have scores of religious women and churches on every corner, and yet not see a whole lot of change in our cities and communities. It is not my intent to beat up on women and make us feel worse than we already do. But it is my mission to expose the enemy in our camp. In so doing, I must sometimes be blunt and honest about the current state of affairs.

The information presented in this book is meant to bring conviction to the reader, to wake you up, to give you the desire to get out from under the plan of the enemy. It is also intended to give practical steps for moving in a new direction. Guilt and condemnation are not the goals. Yes, together we can acknowledge that we have succumbed to the enemy's plan for too long. As we understand what has happened and realize there is a way out, we can decide to embrace the ways of God. We can actually get up and begin to walk in victory!

It is time for the Body of Christ to rise up and be the army of the Lord who will make a difference in the realm of the Spirit. Women who love God with all their hearts and who have learned to move out of religion into Spirit living will be mightily used by God to tear down and destroy that which has hindered the people of God.

Men must come to that same place in Spirit living. Women and men must work together, but there are some things that women must work through before we can take the place God has for us. That's what this book is about. The things we say in this book are not exclusively for women, but they will enable women to take their places beside men so they can then be used by God, along with others, to build and plant the true Kingdom of God.

I may not say everything you want me to say
I do not say things that have not been said before. I will *not* say some good things that you have already heard many times. I speak as someone who once thought she was pleasing to God because of knowledge and ability, not realizing that God was not impressed because I was not listening to His voice.

Some people may feel I should put more emphasis on reading, studying, or memorizing scripture. I do believe a knowledge of the Word is important. We have to know what God says to obey Him. But I have found that many people equate a knowledge of the Word with pleasing God. This country has millions of people who know the Word of God, who are forever learning, but never coming to a knowledge of the Truth. The first-century church did not have the Bible as we know it today, but they were able to accomplish something we don't seem to be able to do—they turned the world upside down. So the emphasis will not be on what you know, but on what you do.

Others may be disappointed that I do not give attention to their favorite spiritual gift or power. Once again, I think Spirit living is more than spiritual gifts. Of course, I believe both the gifts and fruit of God's Spirit are important. Spiritual gifts do not impress me if the life behind the gifts is not filled with God's love and peace. So while a lot of people esteem gifts, that will not be my focus.

The focus in this book is to move us from carnal living to spirit living. I am very excited about the marvelous things God is currently doing. I believe we may very well be on the verge or the fringe of a major revival. But what I have noticed over the years and from a study of revival, carnality is the main hook the enemy uses to destroy revival. If we don't make the proper distinction between carnality and spirituality, our ignorance will give place to the enemy.

We each have the opportunity to be a pacesetter; to be a forerunner if we take this challenge today and go for it. I challenge and admonish you to offer yourself fully surrendered to God to work a new thing in you.

The Carnal Christian

You might carry a big study Bible with you everywhere you go
Everybody is impressed with the amount of Scripture you know
But if you only know in your head and your life does not show
You're just a Bible-toting, Bible-quoting carnal Christian

If at every signs and wonders meeting, you're on the front pew
Everybody is glad when you pray in a language you never knew
But if with all your power, you don't obey what the Spirit says do
You're just a miracle-seeking, tongue-speaking carnal Christian

Change is what it is all about. God wants to push back the tide of the enemy's operation in our lives and in the world. God wants to work a change in our lives. Will you be one to receive the light of Jesus (or a recharge of the light you may have received before)? Then say to God:

Prayer:
Father in heaven, it is my desire that my life would be pleasing to You. Help me to understand where I am in this journey of walking in Your Spirit and spiritual maturity. Perhaps I am not as far along as I thought. Maybe I am further along than I give myself credit for. Whatever the case, I leave all of my preconceived ideas right here and ask You to show me how to go on from here. Light or rekindle a fire within me and burn off outer crusts of my life so the light and fire of Jesus might be seen in me.

CHAPTER 2

Movin' Beyond Worthlessness

"Behold, the handmaid of the Lord; be it unto me according to thy word."

Luke 1:38

I WAS RAISED IN A CHRISTIAN home. My parents were missionaries at Cedine Bible Mission in Tennessee. Christian camping for black Americans was the major focus of the mission while I was growing up. I was third in the line of six children. I truly am thankful to God for the family I was brought up in. One advantage of being raised by parents who were also missionaries was that I was presented with the claims of Jesus Christ very early. I asked Christ into my heart at the age of five.

At the same age, Satan began to plant his seeds of destruction in my life. At the age of twelve, Jesus stepped in and rescued me from the clutches of the enemy. Also at the age of twelve, I was led to recommit my life to the Lord. I wondered if I really understood what I had done at the early age of five.

At sixteen, I was confronted by God in a major way. In the spring of my junior year in high school, Butch Upton, a former missionary to New Guinea, who had also become a Christian through Cedine Bible Mission, loaned me a book entitled *Rees Howell, Intercessor*. After reading the book, I knew God wanted me to give my everything to Him unconditionally. But I was not sure if that was what I wanted to do. I felt that at sixteen, I still had my life ahead of me and if I let God take complete control at that point, it would mean He would get to choose my career, whether I would marry of not, and all sorts of things. I was not quite sure I wanted God to make those decisions for me. In fact, giving up the right to get married was a major obstacle in my mind.

I remember God used Tom Skinner, one of the speakers at camp that summer, to challenge me with new insights about the Kingdom of God. It was after much anguish and prayer that I finally decided to give God unconditional surrender. This happened the fall of my senior year in high school, just before I turned seventeen. It had taken me about six months to count the cost of that offer. When I said, "Yes, Lord," my life was no longer my own but His to do with as He pleased. I would let Him do any and all that He would desire to do in me. I agreed that I would let Him run my life, choose whether or not I would marry, choose my career, where I would live, and the whole bit.

I need to emphasize that God wooed me to Himself. I did not initiate giving my all to God. I argued with Him, but somehow over the six months I was convinced that giving Him complete control was the thing for me to do. Telling God I was giving Him full control was something I did at about seventeen years of age, but letting Him have it took another seventeen years.

Initial decision did not bring reality

Sometimes we forget that there is a process to get us to where we want to go. The decision to do or be something should give us what we need to hold on through the hard times until we make it. If the decision is well thought out and made, counting the cost, nothing should deter us from seeing it to completion. But, we often forget that the decision to be a Christian completely controlled by God is just the beginning of a very long, hard journey.

As I mentioned, that journey took me seventeen years. I am not proud of the length of time it took for me to come to a place that I can say that I was wholly God's. I don't think it has to take that long. But even after those initial seventeen years, God had more He needed to teach me to keep me on the path. I had gotten off the path so many times in those years. One of the reasons was because I did not understand the value God had placed on me.

Satan does not love and esteem women

Satan's job is to keep us thinking that we are worth less than the true value God has bestowed on us. Something that is treasured and valued is treated royally. Something that is devalued is treated like dirt. Satan, unfortunately, has seen to it that many women are treated like dirt. Consequently, we devalue ourselves in our own minds. The way women are treated is directly related to Satan's purpose to destroy our concept of our own worth, and—more importantly—to destroy our ability to live out God's purpose for our lives.

Satan's attacks against us are aimed at our bodies, minds, emotions, reputations, wills, relationships, finances, and possessions. He uses both circumstances and people to attack us. But his dirtiest work is to build within us a mind-set that we are worth less because we are women. That is an improper understanding of the worth God places on our lives.

My heart is overwhelmed at times when I hear of the pain, abuse, and suffering some of my friends and many other women go through. Disease, severe disappointments from children, lack of eligible committed Christian men, husbands who walk out, discrimination on the job, poverty, verbal abuse, emotional abuse, physical abuse, and much more seem to be the plight of many African American Christian women at one time or another. All of this affects what we think of ourselves.

In *Chosen Vessels*, we devoted a whole chapter to the real enemy of women, Satan. Satan hates women, and in his hatred he targets women for pain and hurt.

Satan targets women in particular because they are the keys to change in families. It makes sense to target the key on which families, and thus communities, cities, and the nation rest. By attacking women, he can make the whole nation ineffective to destroy his kingdom.

Satan Targets Women

Women who hurt a lot have difficulty with forgiveness. That's the ultimate purpose of Satan. He knows if we harbor bitterness and unforgiveness in our lives, we will not be properly aligned with God.

Women go through a lot of pain due to a spiritual conspiracy. Men who do not understand the worth of women will easily fall into the hands of Satan, allowing themselves to be used as tools in the attack on women.

Many men do not understand a woman's worth. A man who has been hurt by a particular woman may take it out on all women. The woman who hurt him was probably wounded by a male herself. It becomes a vicious cycle. Both men and women keep the cycle going because we don't understand the real perpetrator behind it all.

Perhaps a look at a conversation between Lucifer and his cohorts, as imagined by Victoria Johnson in her book, *Restoring*

Broken Vessels: Confronting the Attack on Female Sexuality, will help us see where this all began.

One demon had just given a plan of how they could use an attack on women's sexuality to keep women away from a close communion with God. A demon named Jealous says:

> "Without trust in God, she will not be close to God. She will not be able to hear Him warn her of our plans. She will not bring Him into her affairs. She'll just try to handle things on her own. Plus, we can make sure she passes this distrust along to her seed so they won't hear God, either.

> "We'll use our bitterness, unforgiveness, and hate troops. I believe we can actually have a vicious cycle of hate going—women hating men and men hating women. We'll use men in our plan. Since men like power, we'll trick them into using it to oppress and damage women." Jealous paused again to let his words sink in. Then he added, "Don't worry. The men will help us."[1]

That imaginary conversation is just one person's idea of how the vicious cycle of mistrust between the sexes might have begun. We don't really know what actually took place. But today we all can see the obvious results: hate, distrust, abuse, bitterness. All that can cease when we decide it is important to take the necessary steps to go God's way rather than continuing to fall into Satan's traps.

Worthy in God's eyes

It is hard to have a proper understanding of God's value on our lives if we have a false conception of God's love or if we think he has relegated us to dead-end functions in His Kingdom. Being raised in a Christian home, I had heard of God's love from day one. It took more than thirty years before I understood that love as a unique gift for me. I had an intellectual understanding of the love of God, but because of circumstances, observations, and experiences, I could not understand that kind of love on an emotional level.

My concept of God was that though He may love me, He actually loved those of other races more. In my subconscious, I also thought He loved men more than he loved women. My sense of self-worth reflected society's values and estimation of my worth. Now, I don't think I ever consciously thought those exact thoughts; but when the light of God's love finally broke through to me, I realized that these thoughts had been lurking in the shadows of my emotions for years.

God, in His love and mercy, pursued me, showing me His love, telling me that He had good plans for me, assuring me that He wanted to use me as a chosen vessel. I resisted His pursuit, because I did not believe I was worthy of God's love or His use.

When I began to hear God saying He wanted to use me in His service, I had a really big problem with it. First, I did not believe God called many African Americans. I certainly had not seen many African Americans in ministry outside of pastoring or teaching in local churches. That was long before ministers such as John Perkins, Tony Evans, Clarence Walker, Jr., T. D. Jakes, Myles Monroe, Willie Richardson, Haman Cross, Jr., and others wrote books or came into national prominence.

Secondly, based on my theological upbringing, I had serious doubts that He called women to visible roles of service. Having seen few African American men in ministry, I hardly need mention the even smaller numbers of African American women I'd seen in ministry. Yet I sensed God's hand and call upon my life. It left me in quite a dilemma. That dilemma, combined with a deep-rooted belief that God did not love me as much as He loved others, took some time for me to work out.

When I look back, I can see that God had been trying to tell me for some time that He loved and wanted to use me. I never believed He was talking to me. My self-concept did not fit with what I was hearing God say to me. I thank God for His persistence. Finally, I did realize that *Yes, Jesus loves me!*

I also had to realize that God's use of people did not always mean visibility. God began to show me that the often hidden ministry of intercession was of great value and worth in His kingdom. Prayer was the real work.

Satan's attack brings feelings of worthlessness

The difficulty I had in understanding God's love for me and His purpose for my life was the result of a well-planned conspiracy by God's number one enemy. As long as I felt inferior as a person, and as long as I had a complex about my gender—believing God loved men more than he loved women—Satan could cheat me out of God's love and thereby prevent me from fulfilling God's purposes. Satan knows that love is as strong as death. He does not want me to know the love God has for me. God's love gives me the strength and power to overcome and defeat Satan's deadly tactics:

> *Put me like a seal over your heart,*
> *Like a seal on your arm.*
> *For love is as strong as death,*
> *Jealousy is as severe as Sheol;*
> *Its flashes are flashes of fire,*
> *The very flame of the Lord.*
> (Song of Solomon 8:6)

Because of the power of love, Satan seeks to destroy my recognition of God's love for me, my love for God, and the love God shows to others through me.

Now that I know the satanic origin of my previous mind-set of inferiority, I do not have to continue to believe lies. I can accept the truth of God's Word, which is:

- I am accepted in the beloved (Ephesians 1:6).

- I have been chosen as a vessel of honor (2 Timothy 2:21).

- God loves *me* (John 3:16).

As for the pain I may have experienced at the hand of the enemy, I now look at it all in a different light. I can exchange the pain for glory. I can bask in the love of God that heals me from the pain of rejection I endure as a woman. I can rejoice in the fact that, by God's grace and the works that He has ordained for me to walk in, I will defeat the enemy. In recognizing the hatred between Satan and women as mutual, I can now:

- become a better partner with God;

- enter God's war room for strategies;

- resist Satan with a more perfect design to destroy his work; (1 John 3:8).

Our problem: our own image

To many women, it appears God has placed them low. Many women think far less of themselves than the worth God has placed on them. In the book *Chosen Vessels*, we spoke of how women are highly esteemed by God and, because of their value, placed in a protected place in the home under their husbands.

It is important to understand that God does not place women under *all* men just because they are women. The married woman is under *one* man, her husband. The husband's job is to cover her, to treat her as royalty, and to love her sacrificially, as Christ loved the church to the point of giving Himself up for her (Ephesians 5: 22-29). A wife's life in turn brings honor to her husband. This is the ideal.

Many of us have to settle for less than the ideal with the men in our lives. But we must not lose hope. To unmarried women and married women alike, I urge you to look to Jesus. He will treat you like a queen as He anchors and sustains your heart.

God made His love real to me through my husband and the many friends He gave me in the Body of Christ. It did not matter how long and hard Satan had ruled over my thoughts of my-self—God's love and light broke through.

God is calling women to an important work

In a corporation, a person's financial worth is determined by what the person can bring to the company. A chief executive with much experience in running profitable companies can make a salary of millions in one year. In the sports arena, the star whose skills help a team win will be worth millions. In God's Kingdom, women have immeasurable worth because we have been chosen to defeat God's number one enemy. Enmity was placed between Satan and women (Genesis 3:15). The primary way we overcome this enemy's plan of death is by using prayer. This is God's plan. Nothing else will bring the change we all desire to see. Building more churches will not do it. Preaching more sermons will not do it. God is looking for women to take up His call to prayer. Much of the pain, rejection, and abuse at the hands of whomever Satan uses is designed to keep us away from an intimate and communing relationship with God. It is to keep us from the power of prayer.

God wants to change our lives by lifting us above the pain. Understanding the awesome value of prayer and the place women have in prayer in God's Kingdom will lift us above pain and abuse. It's difficult to maintain a consistent, fervent prayer life if you doubt God's love, devalue your worth, or do not understand the awesome power and place of prayer.

We cry out, "Why, Lord?" We ask, "when will we be avenged of our enemy?" not understanding that the human enemy we speak of often is just a tool of the real enemy. Our focus has been on flesh and blood, not on the spiritual beings behind the physical. We have not yet cried out day and night to be avenged of our spiritual enemy.

We will be avenged of our real enemy when we understand the purpose and power of prayer and how prayer is tied in to our destiny as women. God can use a woman to teach and preach. (We'll discuss women in ministry in another chapter.) But a person's worth in the kingdom has little to do with the ability to speak to humans. In fact, if I read my Bible correctly, everybody has worth in the Body. The parts of the body that we consider less honorable, actually have honor in abundance.

> Nay, much more those members of the body, which seem to be more feeble, are necessary: And those members of the body, which we think to be less honourable, upon these we bestow more abundant honour; and our uncomely parts have more abundant comeliness. For our comely parts have no need: but God hath tempered the body together, having given more abundant honour to that part which lacked: That there should be no schism in the body; but that the members should have the same care one for another. (1 Corinthians 12:22-25)

If preaching and teaching alone could have avenged us of our enemy, we would have been avenged long ago. A lot of preaching and teaching sounds good. Much of it feeds our minds. Some of it touches our emotions and some inspires us to consider doing better. But the preaching and teaching that has the impact to actually change individuals and situations has to come from God's

Spirit. That kind of preaching and teaching has to be sustained by someone's prayers!

Many of the great preachers and teachers whose words sparked revival—such as Finney, Spurgeon, and Moody—had people in their camps whose sole ministry was to pray for them and their services. Prayer is the key. Prayer changes things. Preaching and teaching can change things too, but only if someone is praying. I believe one's worth in the Kingdom of God has much more to do with one's ability to speak to God.

We get a lot of knowledge and motivation from speakers. But there is a lot more life God wants to give to His people through the words of His servants. Don't get me wrong: I appreciate and am extremely grateful for the insight that has come to me from teachers and preachers. And even though I know God is using my own teaching powerfully in many women's lives, I'm not impressed or even satisfied with myself. I am grateful to God that He has been able to use me, but I want to move on up so that His words in my mouth will bring life and spark revival! It's going to take revival to get the enemy out of our community!

A call for all, but especially for women

There is no doubt the ministry of prayer is a calling for every member of the Body of Christ, whether male or female. But I do see in Scripture an emphasis on this call for women.

Satan knows that praying women are an antidote to death's destroying our young. Women in particular are called to an intensity of prayer that goes beyond "now I lay me down to sleep." We need to cry out to God with tears for the needs in our cities. If we don't weep in prayer for our daughters, sons, brothers, husbands and friends, who will? God's antidote to death is praying women.

Consider ye, and call for the mourning women, that they may come; and send for cunning women, that they may come: And let them make haste, and take up a wailing for us, that our eyes may run down with tears, and our eyelids gush out with waters. For a voice of wailing is heard out of Zion, How are we spoiled! We are greatly confounded, because we have forsaken the land, because our dwellings have cast us out. Yet hear the word of the LORD, O ye women, and let your ear receive the word of his mouth, and teach your daughters wailing, and every one her neighbour lamentation. For death is come up into our windows, and is entered into our palaces, to cut off the children from without, and the young men from the streets. (Jeremiah 9:17-21)

That passage of Scripture is calling women. God has given women a destiny to battle for our seed so that strong warriors are developed to destroy the works of the enemy. Instead of being used by the enemy to bring more abuse, God desires to use men and women to love and esteem each other in such a way that we will kick the enemy out of our own lives, out of our families, and out of our communities. We have the responsibility to use the power of prayer in the lives of our loved ones and neighbors.

Other links of prayer ministry to women

There is a need for day and night prayers such as Anna demonstrated in Luke 2:37. Anna, a female and a widow, had a recognized ministry of prayer. Her ministry of prayer had a significant place in the first coming of our Lord Jesus. The intensity of our prayers must increase. Like Anna, we will need to add much more fasting to our praying (Mark 9:29). We need to fast and pray until God answers. We give up too easily.

Jesus wondered, "when I come back, will I find faith on the earth?" (Luke 18:8). More than anything, even preaching and teaching, Jesus linked faith to prayer. In this parable He was speaking of a widow going before an unjust judge.

The two other times when the New Testament refers to day and night prayers, they too actually refer to females—widows (Luke 18:1-8; 1 Timothy 5:3-6). Women have a unique place in the ministry of prayer. Women who are unmarried have a special place. I want to encourage single women to consider this powerful ministry.

We have barely tapped the greatest power known to mankind. If you have not read the first book God had me write, *Chosen Vessels: Women of Color, Keys to Change,* I encourage you to secure a copy and read it. In it, I explain what God taught me about the importance of prayer in women's lives.

Our cities need more women who are trained as prayer warriors. If we put ten percent of the money we now put into building houses of brick and mortar into equipping women to build themselves into houses of prayer, God would do more than visit and touch us, His presence would dwell in our midst. Persistent and fervent prayer will bring to bear the power of God that can bring change. Prayer will change what women think of themselves. Prayer will change the circumstances of our lives.

God will be faithful to His Word. We must not give up. In order to break the cycle or curse on some lives, it may take the prayers of a wife, a mother, sisters, grandmothers, aunts, sisters in the church, and then some. It's going to take united, persistent, prevailing prayer to bring the change that is needed. That's okay. We can join together and do it.

Be it unto to us according to Thy Word

"Be it unto me according to thy word," illustrates the response of a woman who had been called by God to fulfill a great destiny. Mary, who was espoused to Joseph, responded with those words when she was told that she was highly favored of the Lord and that God desired to use her to bring forth a man child into the earth to fulfill His promise that the seed of woman would bruise Satan's head. That promise, or threat, was given to Satan in Genesis 3:15.

It is significant to note here that God gave a woman the greatest task He ever had or will have for a human being. No Old Testament prophet, no New Testament teacher, apostle, elder, evangelist, or prophet would ever have an assignment as great as Mary's task. Without Mary's faithfulness to her call, much of the work of the great men and women of the Old and New Testaments would have been in vain.

God considered Mary a woman of great worth. He shows the same consideration for other women. Mary, the mother of Jesus, symbolizes the many other women who have received God-given opportunities to fulfill great destinies. Could it be we have not understood the significance of our call? If we women understand the great calling that God has placed upon us, we will not want anything more than to pursue the call. Like Mary, each of us can say, "Be it unto me according to your Word, Oh Lord. I want to move on up so that I can fulfill your call on my life."

Women need to spend much time alone with God, solidifying our relationship with Him, becoming grounded and settled in the value He has placed on us. We can then emerge from that intimacy with a renewed sense of worth and purpose.

Prayer:

Lord, forgive me for believing the lie that I was worth less than the value you have placed on me. Thank you that because of the blood of Jesus, I am precious in your sight. Thank you that you have placed the treasure of your Holy Spirit within me. I realize that in myself there is no good thing, but you have made me the righteousness of God in Christ Jesus. Teach me to walk worthy of the Lord Jesus unto all pleasing, being fruitful in every good work, and increasing in the knowledge of God. Strengthen me with all might, according to Your glorious power, unto all patience and long-suffering with joyfulness. Thank you! (Colossians 1:10, 11)

CHAPTER 3

Movin' On Up in Purpose

"This is the purpose that is purposed upon the whole earth."
Isaiah 14:26

D O WOMEN HAVE A PURPOSE ON the earth? What are the purposes of women in the most important enterprise in the world—the Kingdom of God? Sometimes, when you look around, it appears that our purpose is to cook the church dinners, clean the church building, or take care of the babies. Not to say that these jobs are not important, but is that all there is? Is that all God has called us to do?

Satan has orchestrated a conspiracy, first against the bride of Christ, and then against women who are members of that bride. Women have lost their purpose. They do not understand the power of prayer that we talked about in the last chapter. Many do not even know God has called them. I had trouble understanding the Lord's call on my life. I answered God's call to work in His kingdom at the same time I gave my life to Him unconditionally. But even then I did not know what a call to serve Him meant.

How Satan sought to steal my purpose

Almost immediately after I gave myself to God unconditionally, the enemy stepped in seeking to destroy me physically by striking me with a rare and usually fatal blood disease. Though the enemy sought to destroy, the hand of God was upon my life. God was never too late in getting me to a doctor or getting me to a hospital. I always got the help I needed when I needed it.

The disease was so rare that many doctors did not know about it. By God's grace, when I was transferred to the University Hospital in Knoxville, Tennessee, a doctor there happened to be familiar with the disease. Satan then took off his gloves and gave it the best shot he had—internal hemorrhaging, stroke, coma, and paralysis. In the natural, NO HOPE. The doctor said in the event I did survive, I would be brain damaged, a vegetable.

When asked by the local paper what could be done, my parents requested prayer. A call for prayer for me went out through the news media. I received cards from all over the country from people who prayed for me. Through the prayers of many others, God's grace and mercy were made evident in my life. God miraculously healed me. When I left the hospital two months later, even the doctor acknowledged that it was a miracle.

It seemed as soon as God gave me a victory, the enemy stepped in to give me a defeat. When I realized I had almost died, I had many questions concerning why and how this could have happened. Hadn't I given my life to the Lord? Why had He allowed this? Because I did not understand, the enemy was successful in getting me to fall into a trap of depression.

The media paid a lot of attention to my plight. I received visits from some of the University of Tennessee athletic teams; prayer vigils and benefits were held on my behalf; and as I mentioned, I received hundreds of cards from around the nation. With all of that attention, I fell into the trap of pride. I actually began to take credit where credit was not due. If anybody should be tempted to take credit, it should have been the hundreds, perhaps thousands who prayed for me. I could not even pray when I needed it the most, because I was in a coma.

Looking back, it really seems stupid, but God used that experience to expose a real stronghold of pride in my life. I wish I could say that I don't struggle with pride anymore. But I can't. I can say that His strength is made perfect in my weakness. I can say that knowing that pride is a weakness for me makes me lean more heavily on Jesus in the strength of His Holy Spirit in that area. And I can attest to God's abundant grace to me in times of need.

I had applied and was accepted to North Park College in Chicago, Illinois at the beginning of my senior year in high school, right before I became ill. I was not able to finish my last year of high school or receive my diploma due to the illness. The college allowed me to enroll anyway. The Lord's keeping power was upon me as I attended college. But in some ways, the intensity of His claim upon my life was relaxed. What I mean by that is while I attended church, fellowshipped with Christians, lead a morally clean life, and even led some student Bible studies, I was more absorbed in nursing books than in the things of God. After many tests, textbooks, and long nights of study, I graduated from college.

The summer I finished college, however, God reminded me of the commitment I had made five years earlier. From that summer, He led me on a journey of reading. The first book I remember that significantly changed my thinking process was *The Normal Christian Life* by Watchman Nee. It was then I first became aware of the fact I was not where I should be spiritually. Now, don't get me wrong— by all of my previous measures, I was a good American Christian. I read my Bible; I did not smoke, drink, dance, or run around. Naturally, I compared myself to others and came out looking pretty good. I was shocked to discover that playing it by the rules does not make someone a good Christian.

I began to realize Christianity was a life source issue, not a list of do's and don'ts. I was pretty good at the do's and don'ts, but I was not too sure if the source of my strength was myself or God. I wanted everything God wanted, so I began to ask Him to do what He needed to do in me so that I might live by His strength. My thinking had been patterned to believe that the up and down walk was the norm and a victorious, joyous, fulfilled walk was just some out-of-reach ideology.

That first summer after college, God gave me a thirst for all that had been provided for me in Christ Jesus. It was during this time that the Lord really began to teach me about prayer and walking in intimacy with God. He began to deal with me about revival. I devoured Nee, Andrew Murray, books on revival, and books about Charles Finney. I read E.M. Bounds, R.A. Torrey; I read about the spiritual giants Mueller and Moody. I was growing by leaps and bounds. In fact, I was learning to walk in the Spirit.

Of course, the enemy was not just casually observing my pursuit for spiritual things. He set a number of different traps and trip-ups. One trip-up was to get me to take the issue of life partnership back into my own hands. When I took it off the altar and back into my own hands, Satan began to work havoc. Finally, after enough beating up, I gave it back to God.

Beginning of understanding my purpose

I was single and working full-time, free to spend all excess money on books. When I read a good book that blessed me, I naturally wanted to share it. So I would buy two or three copies at a time and give them away. At this time, the Lord had blessed me with two close friends, Brenda and Elois. We fellowshipped, shared, and grew together. We leaned on each other for prayer support. Those times of fellowship were very precious for each of us. I don't believe I would have maintained stability in the things of the Lord without them. Even today, though we have gone our separate ways and actually live in three different cities, we still get together at times and pick up where we left off.

Looking back, I can see I was being used of God to challenge and motivate others. I was not really aware of that happening then.

The walk in the spirit was just a natural overflow of a life in communion with God.

In the midst of everything, in the back of my mind was the plaguing question, "Why are there so many ups and downs?" Victory came first and then defeat. I was led to study in the book of Acts and that made me even more discouraged as I became more and more aware of the difference between the early church and what I saw around me.

The Lord led me to see His heart and concern for the body of Christ. He showed me how nothing less than an awakening, a revival, would solve the ills of the church, or, indeed, the ills of the world. He called me to pray for revival. He reaffirmed what He had begun to show me the year I had finished college. He continued to give me insight concerning revival.

I began to understand the place of prayer in the call the Lord had placed on my life. I felt the Lord show me that His hand had been on my life from a young child. I continued in my schooling by way of books and tapes. I walked in and out of traps. I would grow some, stagnate some.

When I began to understand the call God had placed on my life, I guess I thought I would walk in it right away. I ran from the call somewhat. Some things I refused to be involved in. I didn't mind a closet prayer ministry; but there were other things associated with prayer I could do without.

But after becoming comfortable with a ministry of prayer, with speaking to God, I became aware that He also wanted me to speak to others as well. First, I struggled big time with insecurity, fear, and low self-esteem. Getting up in front of people was almost impossible for me. "Okay, Lord, if that's what You want, You'll have to provide abundant grace." That's exactly what He's done. But there were other issues. I wanted a normal family life. I had grown up in a "ministry family" and knew firsthand the pain of being a PK and a MK (preacher's kid and missionary's kid).

In the midst of the Lord teaching me, I met Uwaifo, and we got married. By the leading of the Lord, my husband and I started a book ministry. That ministry really began when I bought books and gave them away. But with a distribution company, I was able to influence more people by recommending books and making them easily accessible. We did home book parties and book tables at conferences. At last, I began to see the purposes God had for me. But Satan still had one of his biggest traps waiting for me. We'll pick up on that in the next chapter.

Purpose

It is important to understand God's original purpose for women if we are going to fulfill it. Understanding and fulfilling our purpose will allow women to rise above abuse and misuse. As Myles Munroe says in his tape series, "Principles of Purpose," "When the purpose of something is not known, abuse is inevitable."

God loves and esteems all women. God will make real His love for us because He wants women to fulfill His purposes. Women have an important role as partners with God.

Men, too, need to understand God's purposes for women and how Satan has tried to sabotage that plan. The purpose of males, whether sons, fathers, husbands, or brothers in Christ, is tied up in the purpose of females. When men fall into Satan's traps of abuse and misuse of females, they do not receive the support; prayers, encouragement, words of peace, godly influence, and loving service they require to fulfill their own destinies.

God has provided a cycle of healing. As Christ commended His love toward His Bride, men commend their love toward women, who in turn bless men with prayers and help. This cycle overcomes the enemy's tactics.

"Why do we always have to be the ones to fix things?" ask many women. "Why can't we just wait for the men to get it together?" To those of you who wonder that, I say this: God is making women an offer, the same offer He is making to men. "Come on up beyond religion to Spirit living. Be my partner to start a new cycle." It does not matter who takes His offer first.

What are we waiting for? Let's go for it. This is not about women versus men. It's about breaking a cycle that is destructive to both men and women. It's about men and women helping each other to be what God wanted us to be in the first place.

Women are demonstrators

God has given most women communication skills. Women like to talk. My husband will sometimes comment on how long I've been on the phone with a girlfriend. It's inconceivable to him that we would have things to talk about for that length of time. He can say what he needs to say in a couple of minutes.

Women were designed with unique verbal skills. A woman's brain is different from a man's brain. Men are not as verbal as women. That's no revelation, but what women often do not consider is that *because* men are not as verbal, they do not respond to words the way we do.

Because women have a way with words, we sometimes think we can use our communication skills to change men. No matter how often women try to use words to change the men in their lives, it doesn't work. Words will change *women*. Most of the time, words from women will not change men. In fact, if you think about it, most women respond readily to the words of men. Some men know they can use words to talk their way into the lives of women. Women then later kick themselves because they fell for someone who was just a smooth talker.

While men do not respond as readily to the words of women as do women, they do respond more readily to the spiritual realities they see. Because they are visually oriented, they will change spiritually when they observe women walking in the Spirit. We can try to talk to men until we are blue in the face, but many will not hear us. But if we just begin to live it, our behavior will draw them to Jesus.

I like what Mary Jean Pidgeon says in her book, *We've Come a Long Way Baby!*:

> One of God's purposes for men to be attracted to women is to draw men into the matters of the heart. Another purpose is so he will be willing to reproduce. Another is to motivate him visually toward holy living. When a man is attracted to a Christ-centered woman, she has power to lead him into spiritual purity, producing a cleansing effect on his life . . . . As the man watches the woman, she is able to influence him into spiritual growth and to motivate him toward spiritual purity.[1]

This is one purpose for women in God's economy of things. By a woman's example and influence, she will positively affect the men in her life. The woman is to *do* the Word, not try to use words.

We have clear precedence in Scripture for these instructions. We are to be doers of the Word and not hearers only (James 1:22). We are to be quick to hear, but slow to speak (James 1:19). Again, to quote from Mary Jean Pidgeon:

> Generally it is words, spiritual containers, that unlock a woman's mind, whereas a man's mind is unlocked by images. When a man sees a woman living out God's word, he is motivated by the sight of her more than by any words she speaks.[2]

This is exactly the example the Scripture talks about:

Likewise, ye wives, be in subjection to your own husbands; that, if any obey not the word, they also may without the word be won by the conversation (behavior) of the wives; While they behold your chaste conversation coupled with fear. (1 Peter 3:1-2)

Again, we are talking about in the natural realm. When women are in natural relationships with men, the Bible emphasizes what men will *see*, not what they will hear. For many of the men in our lives, whether they are teen or adult sons, brothers, pastors, husbands, bosses, or just brothers in Christ, we need not talk so much *to* them, but live the life before them and talk to the Father *for* them. Then, if we do talk to them, it will be with wisdom. Many times, God would just have them watch our example.

We need to talk to God more and let God talk to them
We need to stop trying to preach, nag, or otherwise change men with *words*. Men need much more than words for a spiritual awakening. Women make up more than 75 percent of the membership of African American churches. For years, women have been trying to get their men to go church. It hasn't worked.

I heard the story of a woman who kept nagging her husband to go to church. He wouldn't go. One day, the Lord spoke to her and told her, "Be quiet. Leave him alone and let me work on him." So she stopped trying to talk him into going to church.

As it turned out, The Lord gave this husband a dream one Saturday night that scared him. The next morning, he woke up and said, "We're going to church today!" If we stop trying to use all of our abilities of persuasion, coercion, manipulation, and judgment and turn our men over to the Lord, He'll do a much better job with them than we ever could.

Jawanza Kunjufu's book, *Adam! Where Are You?: Why Most Black Men Don't Go to Church*, discusses 21 reasons African American men stay away from church. We won't go into all the reasons, but it is significant to note that the number one reason is hypocrisy. In his chapter on solutions, Kunjufu says, "The need for role models who are consistent is important for everyone, for children, adolescents, adults, and elders. It has often been said, 'I would much rather see a sermon than hear a sermon.'" 3

While it is disturbing that so many of our male loved ones shun church, we need not worry about that right now. For the most part, what goes on in church has to do with *words*. That's why many churches attract a majority of women: we like words. Although many of the reasons given for negligent church attendance are things that only revival will rectify, women walking in God's power can be instruments in bringing that revival. As we move beyond religion to Spirit living, I believe change will of necessity take place in our churches.

Men want to *see* spiritual life. They will be involved where and with whom they can see and partake of life. Women have the responsibility to demonstrate spiritual life, not just in the church, but in our homes and communities. It is much easier to talk about spiritual life than to live it out, especially in a hostile environment. But that is the essence of our destiny.

As we grow in Spirit living, learning to be demonstrators of spiritual life, the sky will be the limit to our ability to use spiritual weapons to effect change. Without a full recognition of our purpose, we might get trapped in religion.

What about men?
Doesn't God give men some responsibility in life? The answer is yes; God gives men much responsibility. Men are instructed to treat women with such sacrificial love that the works of the enemy are destroyed. I pray that God will continue to raise up people who will challenge men to stand up and be men of God. I thank God for men like Tony Evans, T.D. Jakes, and Haman Cross, Jr. (the

pastor of the church I attend) and many others who are speaking out to recover among our men that which has been lost. I also thank God for the convicting power of His Holy Spirit, who shows individual men when they have fallen into the enemy's trap. There are men who have, by God's grace, seen the challenge to be faithful men of God and fulfilled it.

My husband is one such man. I thank God for my husband, Uwaifo, who is one of the most godly men I know. He has loved me sacrificially in spite of myself. God used his love to heal me when I was brokenhearted. He has encouraged the gifts and the call God has placed on my life. He has not felt threatened one bit by what God has done through me. He has released me to be all God wants me to be. He is strong, yet gentle. He is firm, yet tender.

My husband is not a minister in the common understanding of the word, but he is a "man of God." Uwaifo, though not perfect, has, by God's grace, been successful in fulfilling the most important ministry any husband has; he has loved me the way that Christ loved the church. However God has been able to use me is a true reflection of my husband's love. He is an excellent father to our children as well.

Let's face it, we all have been quick to blame others for our situations. We need to blame the real enemy and take responsibility for our failure to look at the conflict from a spiritual perspective. We all need to confess that we have fallen short of our God-given destiny. It's not too late to reverse much of what the enemy has done.

Men need the prayers of God-fearing, Spirit-living women to be able to fulfill God's purposes for their lives. As much as we would like to be free from responsibility, we have to accept the responsibility God has given us to pray, to encourage, and to live in the Spirit.

As men and women learn to live spiritually, we will each walk in our purpose. As we mature spiritually, by the grace of God, the Body of Christ will put on the lovely garments of praise and the boots of authority to put God's enemies under our feet (Matthew 22:44; Romans 16:20; 1 Corinthians 15:25; Ephesians 1:22). We are in union with Christ, his Son, who defeated the Devil. We are a bride in combat boots!

Prayer:

Father, I give you permission to bring me into Your purposes. I want to be an effectual stone in Your house of prayer. Forgive me for focusing on others when I have no control over them. I confess my denial of Your power. Teach me to be strong in You and in the power of Your might.

SECTION II

Roadblocks to Spirit Living

CHAPTER 4

The Religion Trap

"Having a form of godliness, but denying the power
thereof: from such turn away."

2 Timothy 3:5

WE HAVE ALREADY ESTABLISHED that when women live lives in dependence upon the Spirit of God, by our actions we *demonstrate spiritual living*. Spiritual living is *not* demonstrated by words, or by participation in religious activities. It is far easier to talk spiritual talk and to be involved in religious activities than it is to live the spiritual walk. Many women are religious—that is, they talk and participate but they are not spiritual. They do not live the Word. They may know a lot, but their knowledge is not a way of life.

I will not minimize the change God has made in individual lives, but I want to see more change in our communities. I want to see crack houses close down. I want to see men respect and esteem women, treating them royally. I want to see our prisons empty. God is able to do all of that. He's done it before. My God is able to do exceedingly more than just give us goose bumps as we go about our religious ways (Ephesians 3:20). To see all God is able to do, we have to move beyond religion to Spirit living.

My journey continues

I mentioned it took seventeen years for God to get all that I had surrendered to Him. God did a lot in my life those seventeen years. I learned a lot. I grew a lot. I was learning to live in the Spirit. You can imagine then the surprise I had when towards the end of those seventeen years I found out that I was no longer in the Spirit.

In the midst of learning and growing, God allowed me to experience a major loss that shook up my concept of what it meant to be pleasing to God. In one major respect, it was actually service to God that became the biggest obstacle to my continuing in things of the Spirit.

I told you in the last chapter that God lead us to start a book selling ministry. It was a business, but we never made any profit; however, many lives were helped. We saw marriages saved and we saw people get victory in a lot of different areas as a result of being exposed to good Christian literature. I was so happy. God was using me in ministry to others. I was involved with one of the things I loved—books.

But I still fell into a trap. This trap of the enemy was his most cleverly woven one for me to date. Oh, he set this one up well! I walked right into the trap and bang, the door closed. This trap worked the worst damage. I fell to my lowest spiritual ebb. It didn't happen overnight, and by looking at me, most people could not tell that I was living a miserable, defeated life. The most amazing thing is that, though I knew something was wrong, I did not even realize that I had fallen so low and hard until later. I was proud of myself because of my involvement in the ultimate aspect of religion: ministry.

Talk about discontent, despair, discouragement, depression, and debt! Those were my companions. Worries and fears seemed to overwhelm me. I knew it wasn't right, but it seemed I could do nothing about it. The book ministry had indeed become a huge obstacle. At a certain point, I had chosen to look to man for help instead of the Lord. In doing so, I also made an unwise business decision. Eventually, I did not run the company; the company ran me. By getting the foothold, Satan had gotten in the company. The enemy then began to use the company to steal from me. It stole my time with God; it stole my peace; it stole time with my family.

It stole my joy; it stole every ounce of spiritual victory I ever had. It replaced the good things with fears, depression, and the like.

I can look back and see all of this now, but when I was in it, I was blind. I was deceived. I couldn't see the ministry stealing from me; I was blind to my own spiritual condition. The symptoms were there, but I ignored them. One of the reasons I remained deceived is because God was genuinely using the company in the lives of people.

The Lord in his mercy took me overseas away from the company for a few months. That was the beginning of the breaking of the hold the company held over me. I knew God had called me to start the company. I knew He was using it to bless people. So even when He began to allow things to happen that would suggest I should give up the company, I just I couldn't let go. I couldn't give it up. I felt I would be letting God down. Confused and not realizing God himself was calling me to give it up, I resisted God. As a result, I drew closer to the enemy.

I was pretty messed up, but I didn't even know it. I was living on what God had done in my life in the years before. Although the evidence of worry, anxiety, bitterness, inability to pray, lack of peace, and lack of intimacy with God were all around, I did not see the subtle changes. I had changed from an overcoming Christian to a defeated one.

God continued to let the ministry die. I tried to revive it a few times. But finally I did give it up. It was very painful to give up something I loved so much, something I had put so much of myself into, something from which I had received purpose and esteem. It felt as if a part of me died. I did not know what the future held. There was silence when I asked. As far as I knew, I would never be involved with books again.

I think it is fitting to point out that I had no idea how far away I was from God's will and life source. I had found the life in the

Spirit and had lived in it, but grew away from it without knowing it. I also think it should be noted here that the signs of being out of touch with God were there, but it was easier for me to ignore them than to let the truth set me free. The pain of realizing I had slipped so far was too great to face.

In the midst of the crises, I was tempted to take a critical attitude and spirit towards others and what I felt they had done wrong. I have always had a critical attitude. Thank God, He had mercy on me. That critical attitude used to be my lifestyle. If I did not see people with a consistent walk of victory, I would cut them up with my attitude and tongue. Thank God, He helped me see that I need to pray, not criticize. Sure, I slip up from time to time. God has a clever way of making you merciful towards others: He lets you really see yourself. While I was looking at the faults and failures of everyone else, I was blind to my own spiritual condition. I didn't remember the command "If any man thinks he stands, let him take heed lest he fall."

The Lord had to sit me down and get me to remove the log from my own eye. I'll be grateful to God through eternity. He's good. I was nothing! Even my best efforts were just works of the flesh. I secretly thought or hoped I was something. That is why coming to the end of my rope took so long.

A new lease on Spirit living

It was when I dropped to my lowest spiritual state that Jesus stepped into the midst of the darkness of my personal life and offered me light, hope, and all that I had longed for (and quite honestly was deceived into thinking could be achieved by much "religious" activity). At that point, I was forced to admit that in spite of all the "good works" that I had accumulated to my account, I yet lacked the peace, joy, and contentment that the word of God promised.

So at my Father's invitation, I got a fresh start on the journey of living in the Spirit. I soon discovered that journey would not end while I remained here on this earth. This time, the journey involved a lot of changes. During the time after I had finished college when I was first learning to live in the Spirit, I was led to change the attitude (thoughts and feelings) I had about God, about myself, and others.

From the time of the loss of the book business on, the major change that took place in my life was a change in my very life source. I now had to trust God for the ability to obey. In a way, that was much easier than struggling in my own strength to make my own changes or to accomplish His will. But, in some respects, it was more difficult because previously I had so much confidence in my ability to please God. My major difficulty on this latter phase of the journey has been letting go of pride that wants to believe I have the strength and ability to stay on this journey.

I thank God that He has kept up with His end of the bargain. In reality, in the changes in my life, I exchanged my life for His—and I'm really living now!

Many times in the Old Testament the people of God were warned about depending upon the arm of the flesh, in contrast to depending on the help of God (2 Chronicles 32:7, 8). This is ample warning for us to go beyond our tendency to run our lives by the arm-of-the-flesh principle.

The arm of the flesh and Churchianity

The arm-of-the-flesh principle operates when people turn to anything other than God to solve their problems. These would-be sources of help might include intellectual knowledge or strong will and determination. It might be political or social connections. It might be wealth or good looks. It could mean any of a number of things, but it is usually what makes sense to an individual's own understanding to rely upon.

One of the most deadly forms of the arm-of-the-flesh principle is religion that takes a form of godliness, but denies the power of God (2 Timothy 3:5). Religion is *not* a living relationship with a living God. The most deadly religion is false Christianity. There is an authentic Christianity and a counterfeit one. The counterfeit one is what I refer to as "Churchianity." The authentic Christianity and the counterfeit look identical. They both use the same book, the Bible, the same songs and terminology, and even the same mission. The difference is the source of power; with one it is the power of God that passes all understanding. With the other the power source is knowledge; the ability to understand right from wrong.

Counterfeit Christianity involves an understanding of good and evil. Ironically, that understanding may come from a knowledge of God or His Word, but the underlying goal is acquisition of knowledge that makes us self-reliant instead of living moment-by-moment, dependent upon the power of God.

God desires His offspring to live their lives from the Tree of Life as a result of His life in our spirits. It was never intended to be a "knowledge" thing, except for a knowing of God in our inner man that would work its way out to our behavior.

Many sincere Christians try to live the Christian life under the Tree of the Knowledge of Good and Evil. "Churchianity" is based on mental understanding, feelings, and/or a determination to do right. A false understanding of the power source of Christianity can prevent us from an authentic relationship with God. It keeps us away from the protection of God and under the curse of the enemy. "Churchianity" keeps us trying to live the Christian life by the arm-of-the-flesh principle.

The arm of the flesh goes back to the Tree of the Knowledge Of Good and Evil in the Garden of Eden. Rick Joyner in his book, *There Were Two Trees in the Garden*, states:

> Satan did not tempt Eve with the fruit of the Tree of Knowledge just because the Lord has made it taboo. He tempted her with it because the source of his power was rooted in that tree . . . The knowledge of good and evil kills us by distracting us from the One who is the source of life: the Tree of Life—Jesus. The Tree of Knowledge causes us to focus our attention upon ourselves. Sin is empowered by the Law; not just because the evil is revealed, but the good as well. It drives us either to corruption or self-right eousness. Both lead to death. [1]

Something has to change if we're going to see change in our families, churches, and communities. Change will not come until we see the difference between religion and an authentic relationship with God.

The fact that women make up about seventy-five percent of the average African American church makes it imperative to get women to move beyond religion to Spirit living. What a potent force for change in our communities if a host of praying women decided to demonstrate Spirit living! God is looking for strong female spiritual warriors to fight a ruthless enemy.

The arm of the flesh will not be effective in those who have been chosen by God to bring defeat to the works of the enemy of God. It is necessary for women to lean not on their own understanding, but on the will of God. The battle will not be ours, but God's (2 Chronicles 20:15). We will not win the battle with carnal or fleshly weapons (2 Corinthians 10:4-6). Our weapons must be spiritual.

I can challenge you because God has dealt with me personally. As a young woman, in my twenties and early thirties, who was extremely religious, moral, deeply committed, and involved in religious activities, God rained on my parade. I was riding on this merry-go-round of religion, being lulled to sleep and God suddenly snatched me off, shook me, and woke me up.

Though it was uncomfortable when it all happened, I can look back and be glad, because I saw who was really operating the merry-go-round. The enemy is slowly inching the merry-go-round of religion to a cliff of destruction. God is truly merciful to give us all a chance to move beyond mere religion. Let me share the story of how my eyes were opened to the truth.

Personal Testimony

Like most people, I had no idea how far I had fallen from the original purposes of God. I really thought I had it going on with the Lord. I was doing my religious activities: Bible studies, prayer meetings, conferences, and church meetings. I was reading Christian books and listening to Christian teaching tapes, Christian radio and Christian television. At my church, I was superintendent of the Sunday School and a leader in the program for young girls; I also was involved in the evangelistic program. Outside of my local church, I hosted and organized home Bible studies, was involved in a young adult ministry, and was one of the youngest board members of a city-wide women's ministry. No one could have convinced me that I was not pleasing to God. I, no doubt, was proud of how much more pleasing I was to Him than were many others. I was deceived, full of idolatry to the point of idolizing myself.

I was full of talk about the Word and things of the Spirit. I sure knew how to talk! At the same time, I had a lot of hard questions about Christianity and was pursuing answers. I was learning and I believe I was even growing. During the times I was in the Spirit, I grew. I thought I was there all of the time, because my life consisted of so much religious activity.

Looking back, I now realize I only knew how to *visit* the Spirit. I visited the Spirit by going to meetings and by participating in worship and praising God. I visited the Spirit by praying. But I did not know how to *live* in the Spirit. There is a difference. Sometimes people will visit you and think they live with you. However, God wants His people to live with Him and not just visit from time to time! We often visit the Spirit on Sunday morning at church, but by Monday morning at work we move back into the flesh, with our attitudes of complaining or murmuring.

I stayed in the Spirit as a visitor as long as it was convenient. I moved back into the flesh when there was something to worry about or when someone did something to cause me pain. Because of the idolatrous nature of my religious activity (I was depending on the activities, not my relationship with God, to make myself pleasing to God) I was deceived into thinking I was serving God when I was only serving myself.

My rude awakening occurred when God spoke to me through His Word and essentially said I had been weighed in the balance and found wanting (Daniel 5:27). God allowed a painful experience in my life in which He tested me to live out the Word. It was a test to see if I would *do* what I knew. You too can know if you just visit the Spirit by asking yourself if you actually do what the Word says to do, especially when it's something that is not natural, such as praising God in difficult situations instead of complaining. When you find you are not consistently living by what the Word of God says, you know you do not live in the Spirit.

I knew about being kind, tenderhearted, and forgiving to someone who had disappointed me. I had read about praying for someone who despitefully used me . . . overcoming evil with good . . . letting God have vengeance . . . trusting God to vindicate me . . . and not being anxious about things I could not understand or control in my life. I knew the Word on an intellectual level, but I did not live the Word when the test came.

I failed the test miserably. I became depressed. Instead of the love of God, hate and bitterness were evident in my life. I wanted vengeance. I wanted to vindicate myself. I worried about everything and wasted a lot of time trying to make sense out of things. I tried to lean on my own understanding. I did not acknowledge God in all my ways.

I had been saved since I was five years old and had never considered myself mean. But now I found myself thinking of ways to get revenge, to make the person who hurt me suffer.

In the situation I was in, my way of dealing with it turned out to be the way of the flesh. But I was *religious*! That's the irony of it. I never stopped being religious or talking about and participating in spiritual things. But God wanted something very different for my life. God wanted me to live in the Spirit. He began to teach me how to walk and live in His Spirit. I had to relearn all I thought I knew about God. I had to die a thousand deaths. I had to die to the way I thought things should be and to what *I* wanted.

That traumatic experience was the beginning of a change from religion to living in the Spirit. God showed me that instead of judging the person who I thought had treated me so wrong, I was to cover her in prayer so that she would be protected from the enemy. Learning to pray for and speak well of my enemy at the time was a difficult lesson for me. But it was just the beginning of many spiritual realities God taught me over a period of five years. It was a miserable five years of attaining one of the primary aims of the Christian life: death to self.

A lot of change and loss took place in my life over those five years. I had to let go of the book selling ministry my husband and I had started. This ministry had become my life, something in which I had established worth, esteem, and purpose. Because it had never made any profit, it looked like I was a business failure. My reputation was damaged.

I also lost proximity to good friends by moving twice, once to another country and once to another state. The hardest thing for me was having to stay in the United States for five months while my husband and two young children (ages five and two) were in Nigeria. (My children were being taken care of by another woman who was young, probably cute, could speak my husband's language, and certainly could cook his favorite foods better than I. Believe me, I was not happy and did not trust God.)

When we moved to Nigeria in 1985, we had thought it was to be a permanent move. Consequently, we got rid of most of the things we had accumulated. Because of the financial outlay required to make such a move, I had to give up the recent change we had made for me to leave my job and stay at home. In fact, I ended up working a job and a half most of that transitional year.

Finally, I joined my family in Nigeria. By then, the decision had been made that we were going to come back to the States after my husband finished the year's commitment to the company that brought him overseas. However, circumstances forced me to come back to the States before the year was up. Here I was again away from my husband, with two young children, one on the way, homeless—having to bunk with friends for a couple of months—until my husband came back and we were able to settle down and start over again.

In spite of all of the loss—ministry, reputation, home, possessions, friends, family, living standard, control, career, money—in the end, God brought me to a point that I could understand a little of what Paul said in Galatians 2:20: "I am crucified with Christ, nevertheless, I live. Yet, not I, but Christ lives in me and the life which I now live in the flesh, I live by the faith of the Son of God who loved me and gave Himself for me." For five years I was slowly changed from being a knower of the Word to a doer. I was forced to learn to lean on God and really trust Him for many things I did not understand or had absolutely no control over. It was the worst five years of my entire life, but the best of my spiritual life, God worked inside me those five years to grow me up.

Not that I have obtained all that God apprehended for me. But I know a change has taken place within me. I don't argue as much with God when He asks me to do acts of kindness to people who offend me. I have learned to do it knowing that God is working His character out in me.

God has not finished with me yet. I have not suffered anything near what Paul spoke of.

To this very hour we go hungry and thirsty, we are in rags, we are brutally beaten, we are homeless. We work hard with our hands. When we are cursed, we bless; when we are persecuted, we endure it; When we are slandered, we answer kindly.   (1 Corinthians 4:11-13; NIV)

However, if that is my purpose, God will use it for the up-building of His kingdom, for his glory, and for my good. I have no higher aspiration. I want to minister life to others. I do not want to just disseminate good information, stir up people's emotions, or even give inspiring motivational talks. I want to be used of God to bring healing to broken hearts. I want to see lives dramatically changed. I don't necessarily like difficulties. But I do want to go beyond the norm. From what I can see in the Word of God, death has to work in me that life might work in the people I minister to.

> But we have this treasure in earthen vessels, that the excellency of the power may be of God, and not of us. We are troubled on every side, yet not distressed; we are perplexed, but not in despair; Persecuted, but not forsaken; cast down, but not destroyed; Always bearing about in the body the dying of the Lord Jesus, that the life also of Jesus might be made manifest in our body. For we which live are always delivered unto death for Jesus' sake, that the life also of Jesus might be manifest in our mortal flesh. So then death worketh in us, but life in you. (2 Corinthians 4:10-12; NIV)

I also know God will complete what He started in me (Philippians 1:6). "I know whom I have believed, and am persuaded that He is able to keep that which I have committed unto Him" (2 Timothy 1:12). I believe He will finish whatever it will take for me to walk worthy of His call and destiny.

I now see that my purpose is not just talking about things of the Spirit, not just participating in spiritual things, not just visiting the Spirit, but it is actually living there. It is easier said than done, but God has been faithful. God has brought me out. I could not have made it if I had not surrendered to the death God wanted to bring to my self-life.

Now, in the power of God's might, I have changed. The difference is that, through the process of many difficult and trying experiences, I have learned the reality of living like Jesus in the power of God's Holy Spirit. The key is living the Word of God by the Spirit of God. I found I knew a lot, but I did not do all I knew.

An example of learning to do the Word

When God began to teach me Spirit living, one of the lessons was to learn to overcome evil with good (Romans 12:21). That is a hard lesson to learn. And I had to learn it in the arena of a male/female relationship: my marriage.

You may have heard of the book, *Men are from Mars, Women Are From Venus*. Men and women *are* different. Men do and say things that women don't understand. In fact, men have this uncanny ability to say and do things that hurt women. Uwaifo, my husband, who is very sweet, *is a man*, and he has said and done things that have hurt me. I have done the same to him. It's inevitable when two different people from two different cultures who also are from two different planets live together.

When I'm hurt, my natural tendency is to withdraw. In bed at night, my withdrawal is very obvious. I crawl as far to my side of the bed as possible without falling on the floor, wondering if the floor or the sofa might be a better option. Of course, I turn my back toward Uwaifo. Mind you, I already told him that nothing was wrong when he questioned me.

Now, because I am a Christian, I know I will eventually have to forgive him. But I think that I have to give him the silent treatment for at least three days to teach him a lesson. He shouldn't treat me like he did. I have to protect myself.

So there I lay, trying to go to sleep, but sleep wouldn't come. In this situation, God chooses to go to work on me.

In the quietness, I seem to sense a voice speaking to me, "Turn over and scratch his back." "That can't be God," I think. I try to shake it out of my mind. But it won't go away. When I think about it, I realize it certainly cannot be the devil. And I know it's not me. Scratching my husband's back is the *last* thing I want to do at the time. My husband loves to have his back scratched. That would be something nice to do. But remember, he hurt me and I'm mad. I can't be nice to him. I have to punish him.

But the voice won't go away. So I argue, "Lord, it just does not make sense. How will I get him back?" Guess what comes to my mind next? "Vengeance is mine, I will repay" (Romans 12:19).

"But God, I don't understand what scratching his back will accomplish. If I'm nice to him, he'll just think he can talk to me any way he wants to." The answer: "Lean not to your own understanding, but in all your ways, acknowledge me and I will direct your paths" (Proverbs 3:5,6).

"Well, I really don't feel like it. Lord, I'm too weak to do this." The answer: "My grace is sufficient for thee: for my strength is made perfect in weakness" (2 Corinthians 12:9).

"But God . . . ."

"Haven't you been crying out to me to learn to walk in the Spirit? Walking in the Spirit requires you to do as I say regardless of how you think (mind), or what you feel (emotions), or even your desires (will). You can either die to yourself or you can keep yourself alive and thereby lose the life I want to give you" (Mark 8:36).

I truly wanted to learn to walk in the Spirit, but I would rather have learned without having to go through the pain of doing what God told me to do when it was obviously difficult and not at all what I wanted to do. I wished I could get there by just listening to a few more sermons, going to another meeting, having hands laid on me, or reading a couple more books. But that was not how God made it happen.

Much of our religious activity is just that—activity—and not reality. If I had not obeyed those promptings of unconditional love and trusting in God when I could no longer control the things in my life, I would still be out there today searching for more of God in another meeting or book. I got more of God when I had to cry out to God for help to scratch a back that I did not want to scratch. I got more of God when I learned to pray for someone who despitefully used me. I got more of God when I learned to let go of my need to control. I got more of God when I learned to trust Him when things did not go the way I wanted them to go. I got more of God when I learned to let go of the many good things that had become idols or god-substitutes in my life.

God still has much more to do in me. I am currently facing challenges that continue to make me weak and dependent on God. But now I have a different frame of mind going through this new cycle of difficulties. (Thank God, for about five years of peace and rebuilding in between the cycles.) I have seen what God has been able to do through me in the lives of people precisely because of the trials I've undergone. Because I have been forced to be dependent upon God, He is able to do exceedingly abundantly more than all I can ask or think. I am beginning to live out the destiny God has for me by bringing light into the minds of other women. This has not happened by my might (religious activities) or by my power (ability to do good works) but by His Spirit.

As women, Spirit life is a critical part of our purpose and destiny. God wants to enable us to live in the Spirit and to demonstrate Spirit living to others. Just as Satan used a woman to bring mankind out from the protection and blessing of God by the eating of the fruit of the Tree of the Knowledge of Good and Evil, God has chosen women and given them ways of reversing the works of Satan by living in the Spirit and cooperating with God in God-given strategies to bring others into the realm of the Spirit. Women will be used in many ways to bring mankind back into the walk of the Spirit.

Wounded women need God. Most wounded women are seeking God. Many of us at one time or another have fallen into the powerful deception of Churchianity which Satan has put in place to successfully keep us from God's best. When we understand some basic matters of the heart, which we well explore in the next few chapters, we will be able to see how this happens.

Prayer:

Father, I have been too involved in Churchianity, to the neglect of developing a relationship with You. I ask You to judge me on Your scales. Maybe I too have been deceived by religion, thinking I was pleasing You. I don't want to wait until it's too late and all I thought I was doing for You ends up in smoke. Help me to aim my life toward fellowship with You!

CHAPTER 5

The Heart-Tongue Connection

"Woe is me! for I am undone; because I am a man of unclean lips, and I dwell in the midst of a people of unclean lips."

Isaiah 6:5

ONE INDICATION OF WHETHER a person is growing in matters of the Spirit is how she uses her tongue. Matters of one's heart are directly connected to one's mouth. Many people do not understand why they do not use words wisely. Mentally, they may have good intentions, but they will say things that they later regret. In this chapter, we'll explore the basics of how our hearts and tongues are connected.

Out of the abundance of the heart, the mouth speaks (Matthew 12:34)

But those things which proceed out of the mouth come forth from the heart; and they defile the man. From out of the heart proceed evil thoughts, murders, adulteries, fornications, thefts, false witness, blasphemies. These are the things which defile a man. (Matthew 15:18-20)

The passages above show a clear connection between the heart and the tongue. The mouth speaks out of the abundance of the heart. What comes from the mouth comes first from the heart.

The books of Proverbs and Ecclesiastes contrast those who have wisdom of the Spirit to those who are fools. A few passages show how one's words identify a person. For example:

- "He that is perverse in his lips is a fool" (Proverbs 19:1).

- "A fool uttereth all of his mind" (Proverbs 29:11).

- "Excellent speech becometh not a fool" (Proverbs 17:7).

- "Even a fool when he holdeth his peace, is counted wise: and he that shutteth his lips is esteemed a man of understanding" (Proverbs 17:28).

- "A fool also is full of words" (Ecclesiastes 10:14).

In contrast, the wise restrain their words:

- "He that refraineth his lips is wise" (Proverbs 10:19).

- "The tongue of the wise is health" (Proverbs 12:18).

- "The tongue of the wise useth knowledge aright" (Proverbs 15:2).

Other proverbs show the connection between the heart, speech, and wisdom:

- "Wisdom resteth in the heart of him that hath understanding" (Proverbs 14:33).

- "The wise in heart will receive commandments" (Proverbs 10:8).

- "The wise in heart shall be called prudent" (Proverbs 16:21).

- "The heart of the wise teacheth his mouth and addeth learning to his lips" (Proverbs 16:23).

James shows how maturity is related to the taming of our tongues "For in many things we offend all. If any man offend not in word, the same is a perfect man, and able also to bridle the whole body" (James 3:2). We cannot tame our tongues by ourselves, but the Holy Spirit can heal our heart, and our tongues can come under His control as we grow spiritually. Spiritual maturity without a taming of the tongue is a delusion.

If matters of the heart are not dealt with, it is difficult, if not impossible, to live in the Spirit. If you are not spiritually mature everything that comes out of your mouth will have the taste of your soul. Many religious women talk a good religious talk but can easily be drawn into gossip, slander and backbiting. As people in partnership with God to bring blessing, it is important that we do not bring curses, too. It is inconceivable for curses and blessings to come from the same fountain (James 3:11). James tells about a person who has an untamed tongue.

> But the tongue can no man tame; it is an unruly evil, full of deadly poison. Therewith bless we God, even the Father; and therewith curse we men, which are made after the similitude of God. Out of the same mouth proceedeth blessing and cursing. My brethren, these things ought not so to be. Doth a fountain send forth at the same place sweet water and bitter? Can the fig tree, my brethren, bear olive berries? either a vine, figs? so can no fountain both yield salt water and fresh. Who is a wise man and endued with knowledge among you? let him show out of a good conversation his works with meekness of wisdom. (James 3:8-13)

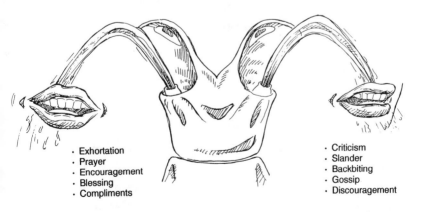

- Exhortation
- Prayer
- Encouragement
- Blessing
- Compliments

- Criticism
- Slander
- Backbiting
- Gossip
- Discouragement

Spiritual anatomy

Let's take a lesson in spiritual anatomy. It will be the foundation for understanding the relationship between the heart and the tongue.

Mankind is a triune being. He is made up of three parts: body, soul, and spirit (see illustration below). Man was formed out of the dust of the earth (body). God breathed into him the breath of life (spirit), and man became a living soul, a being like God, with a mind, a will, and emotions (Genesis 2:7). When the spirit hit the body, the soul was formed. The soul plus the human spirit makes the *heart* of man. The soul (apart from the spirit) plus the body makes the *flesh* of man. Paul's desire is that each believer be wholly sanctified, in spirit, soul, and body (1 Thessalonians 5:23).

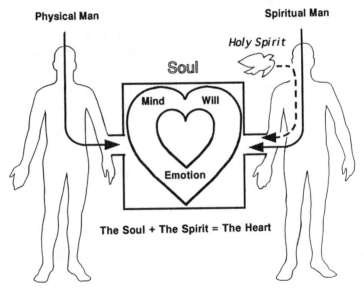

Wisdom is of the Holy Spirit. As our hearts are more in tune with the Spirit of God, it will show up in our speech. The fool is one who speaks out of his soul, void of the wisdom of the Spirit of God. That person's tongue brings destruction. Because the heart houses both the soul and spirit, the Christian woman is able to use her tongue either wisely by speaking from her spirit, or foolishly by speaking only from her soul (mind, will, and emotions).

Whole hearts

The Christian woman is able to grow a wise tongue by maturing spiritually. A whole heart is one in which the thoughts, feelings, and desires of the soul are in accord with the thoughts, feelings, and desires of the spirit. This is only possible through the work of the Holy Spirit in the human spirit and human soul. A whole heart is a state of maturity indicating completeness and soundness throughout a person's entire heart. It is characterized by love, strength, peace, joy, song, and the ability to do right (to love, praise, serve, obey, and seek God) in the midst of any circumstance. The thoughts, desires, and feelings of the heart are in accord with God.

Having a whole heart should be one of our chief aims as Christians. All of our responses to God must come from a whole heart. There is no other way to fulfill God's purposes for us. God tells us to do everything with a whole heart. Among other things, we are to *obey* God from a whole heart, we are to *love* Him with a whole heart, and we are to *seek* Him with a whole heart (Deuteronomy 6:5; Mark 11:29-31; Deuteronomy 11:13; Psalm 138:1; Psalm 111:1; Jeremiah 24:7; Deuteronomy 4:29; Psalm 119:10; Psalm 119:69).

If whole hearts are that important to all of our responses to God, it would make sense to have a clear understanding of what wholeness entails. Let us take a look at a heart that was created whole from the very beginning. The next picture is a visual illustration of what I think Adam's heart looked like when he was created. Pictures only demonstrate concepts; they can never give the true essence of a matter. But despite their limitations, pictures help us understand.

When Adam was first created, his heart was whole, without sin. The Holy Spirit of God overshadowed his heart. He also had a human spirit. His thoughts, desires, and feelings were in keeping with God's ways, since they were not marred by sin. His soul was integrated, whole. At this point in time his mind, will, and emotions were congruent with God's Spirit and with each other. Because Adam's soul had input from the Holy Spirit of God overshadowing him and input from his own human spirit, he was not left to his own resources to behave in a God-pleasing way. I do not believe that God's Spirit dwelled within Adam at this time.

Though Adam was created without sin, God had even better plans for him. God wanted His Spirit to be inside of Adam, not just overshadowing him. So God gave Adam a choice. He could choose to live by God's design, which would be possible if he refused to eat of the Tree of the Knowledge of Good and Evil. He would have then been free to eat of the Tree of Life. Essentially,

Adam was given the choice to live by God's Spirit or by the realm of the soul apart from God's Spirit. God made it very clear that if he chose to eat of the Tree of the Knowledge of Good and Evil, he would die (Genesis 2:17). He would not be allowed to eat from the Tree of Life.

In Genesis chapter 3, the serpent talked Eve into eating of the Tree of the Knowledge of Good and Evil. She in turn convinced Adam to eat the fruit of that tree (Genesis 3:1-8). When they ate, the eyes of both of them were opened and they knew they were naked. They experienced the consequence of their new knowledge.

When Adam and Eve ate of the Tree of the Knowledge of Good and Evil, they became separated from God. A death occurred, and death means separation. At that point, Adam's heart may have looked something like this:

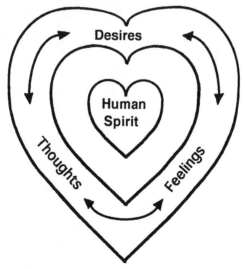

You can see from the picture above that the soul of man was left on its own. It no longer had the input of God's Spirit. The human spirit is still present because a body without a human spirit is dead (James 2:26). But when the human spirit bypasses God's

Spirit and directly inputs into the human conscience, the life of the human soul is diminished. When a person continues to disobey his/her conscience, it is seared and no longer has the input into one's life that it originally had (1 Timothy 4:2).

The soul

The soul is the seat of our behavior. It is made up of the mind, will, and emotions. Our behavior, which includes our speech, comes from our soul (our thoughts, feelings, and desires). This concept is shown below:

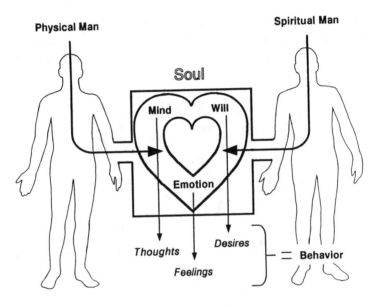

We act and speak according to what we desire or what we think or feel is good or bad. The woman who is led by her soul acts under the Tree of the Knowledge of Good and Evil. Her behavior is not based on the thoughts and ways of God.

We were not designed to live by our soul. We have already mentioned that mankind was made in the image of God. Adam was given a spirit/soul. It is significant that the spirit came first. Mankind was made to live his soul life by the power of his spirit. That was how he was built. The spirit of man empowered by the Holy Spirit of God was designed to lead man, to guide his thoughts, speech, feelings, and desires, and thus his actions. But when man chose to eat of the Tree of Knowledge of Good and Evil, that all changed. He now lived only by his soul, devoid of the life of his human spirit *as led by* the Holy Spirit.

When God saw mankind building the tower of Babel, He commented, "Nothing will be restrained from them, which they have imagined to do." The soul has power. Apart from God, man is still able to accomplish great feats. But that was not the original plan for the creature/Creator relationship.

The original plan was for mankind to live in communion with God and accomplish God's will on earth. The purpose of mankind was not to do whatever he imagined, but to do the will of God. The soul of man was meant to be a servant of the spirit. The spirit of man in connection and subjection to the Holy Spirit of God was to lead mankind. "Those who are led by the Spirit, they are the sons of God." (Romans 8:14) Those who are lead by the Spirit are mature sons, not children tossed to and fro by every wind of doctrine (Galatians 4:1-7; Ephesians 4:14).

Hindrances to Spirit living

Remember, we said God wanted humans to communicate with Him and do His will. That is now possible through becoming a Christian. But becoming a Christian does not make accomplishing God's will automatic. In fact, there are many hindrances to the victorious Christian walk.

One obstacle is our tongues. Our tongues can actually leak Spirit living right out of us. As stated before, we are deluded if we think we have reached spiritual maturity while our tongues are not tamed. No man can tame the tongue (James 3:8). One task of God's Spirit in our lives is to tame our tongues. Changing how we use our tongues is a major focus of growing in the Spirit.

Adam's heart after the fall did not have the wall of God's protection around it. Without the protection of God's Holy Spirit around our soul, the Devil can "get our tongues". The tongue serves as a release valve to the things of the Spirit of God. That's why we are given so much instruction as to the use of our tongues. When we use our tongues in praise, blessings, prayer, and thanksgiving, we will keep our hearts in Christ. But when we use them in slander, curses, complaining, gossip, and the like, we let God's power escape.

Tongue as Release Valve

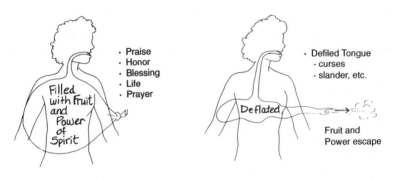

Filled with Fruit and Power of Spirit

- Praise
- Honor
- Blessing
- Life
- Prayer

Deflated

- Defiled Tongue
  - curses
  - slander, etc.

Fruit and Power escape

The characteristics of a whole heart and the hindrances to wholeness listed in the two charts below both have areas that relate to our tongues.

Characteristics of a Whole Heart	Key Verse
Strength	Eph. 6:10
Peace	Phil. 4:7
Joy	Rom. 4:17
Righteousness in any circumstance	Eph. 5:19

Hinderances to Wholeness	Key Verse
Pride	James 4:6
Murmuring and Complaining	I Cor. 4:2
Doubt and Unbelief	Heb. 4:12
Worry	Phil. 4:6
Fear	II Tim 1:7
Sowing to the Flesh	Gal. 6:8
Bad Companions	I Cor 15:33
Evil Speaking	Eph. 4:31

We have established that the status of our hearts determines what comes out of our mouths. We also have stated that our tongues can be tamed only by the Holy Spirit of God. Living or growing in the Spirit will change our tongues. But we have to be careful even when we are growing in the things of the Spirit, because temptations to use our tongues unwisely will constantly be present. We must resist this temptation or the power of the Spirit will be deflated in our lives. We must "keep our hearts with all dilligence because out of it are the issues of life" (Proverbs 4:23).

Prayer:

Father, I want my tongue tamed. The Devil has had it more than I even like to admit. I have used my tongue in gossiping, slandering, criticizing, outbursts of anger, complaining, murmuring and fault finding. Change my heart so that my tongue might be used in giving praise and prayers to You and blessings and encouragement to others.

CHAPTER 6

I'm Broken and I Can't Move Up

"For man looketh on the outward appearance, but the
Lord looketh on the heart."

1 Samuel 16:7

O UR SOULS ARE MEANT TO BE cradled in our spirits. Our
souls were designed to get their life or power source from the
human spirit. The human spirit was designed to get its power from
the Holy Spirit. With the advent of sin into the world, all of that
design was broken.

We now have a break between our soul and our spirit, or a
broken heart. A broken heart is a heart in which all parts of the
soul function separately from the life of the spirit. Unfortunately,
we all come into the world with this primary break. It is shown
below in the illustration of the gap between the spirit of man and
his soul.

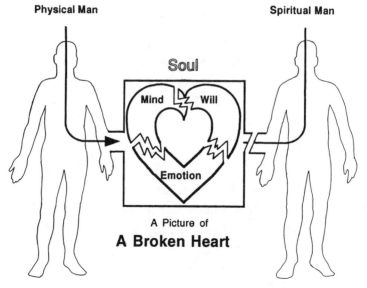

Physical Man

Spiritual Man

Soul

Mind   Will

Emotion

A Picture of
A Broken Heart

There is more than one break, however. The secondary break is the brokenness within the soul itself. Brokenness within the soul occurs when the mind, will, and emotions function separately from each other. A person with this break does things she does not want to do, or things she knows she should not do, or things she does not feel like doing. When our desires, thoughts, and feelings do not work together, our brokenness shows.

I believe everyone will eventually have the second break in their hearts because we all live in a sinful world. Sin is the major cause for the second break (Proverbs 8:36; Jeremiah 30:12-15). A close-up view of the second kind of break is shown below.

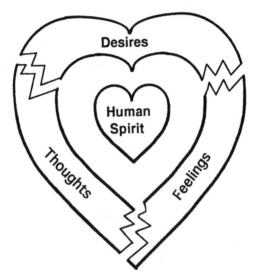

As I look back over the years it took me to become wholly His, I am convinced that a broken heart slowed the process. I had a broken heart, but did not know it. Because of the brokenness, the pieces had to be brought back together. I had to be made whole before I could be wholly His. The break between my mind, soul, and emotions lead me to a faulty understanding of Christianity.

My understanding of Christianity was one that valued the intellect over other parts of my being. Actually, I was lopsided. Not that the intellect was not important, but I had no idea how to be led by the Spirit. I was led by my understanding of God, which included my understanding of His Word. Bible knowledge was a big part of my life as a child. We had to memorize Scripture verses to go to camp. I was involved in Youth for Christ Bible quizzes. Of course, at camp, I heard literally hundreds of sermons. I have always felt safe with an emphasis on intellectual understanding of the Bible. However, I found out that God was interested in my being a doer of the Word and not just a knower.

Because I valued the intellectual and devalued the emotional, I was never in touch with what went on with my emotions. I would try to do the Word out of sheer determination, but my whole heart was not in it. My heart was broken. I knew what to do, but God looked at my whole heart and saw the buried emotions.

There were times when I thought I was obeying God with the full cooperation of my mind and will, but my emotions did not go along with the program. They remained bruised, refusing to participate in full obedience. As a result, I thought I was a good Christian, but was deceived in who I thought I was. Not that God wanted to lead me only by my emotions; the goal of Christianity is to be led by the spirit, empowered by God's Holy Spirit. However, God's Spirit operates in its maximum power through wholeness. Broken hearts are a major obstacle that keep women out of Spirit living.

How I found out I had a broken heart

The following experience made me aware that my mind and emotions were not working together. I thought I had forgiven a friend of mine over a particular offense. But my friend insisted something was not right. I was sure I had forgiven her. I asked God about it. He showed me that I had forgiven her—mentally. He then showed me that I had not forgiven her from my emotional center, because my emotions were separated from my mind. That separation was the result of my broken heart. From that event began my quest to understand broken hearts. My eyes were open to the fact that no matter how much I thought I was obeying God, I was deceived. When I behaved out of my broken heart, I could not obey God with all my heart (Deuteronomy 30:2).

Adam's heart

We have looked at Adam's heart. As human history went on, sin, of course, continued. As sin continued, so did the break in the heart of mankind. Along with sin came a variety of emotions, including shame, as evidenced by the activity of hiding (Genesis 3:10). We also see the emotion of fear from the time of Adam on. These emotions are natural, but without the power of the Spirit of God overshadowing Adam's human spirit, the soul's behavior goes against God. This is the foundation of the break within the soul.

The broken heart shown in the illustration on page 72 also depicts what Cain's heart might have looked like after he killed Abel. That first murder was the result of a soul left to its own devices. In looking at the incident, we see other evidence of the separation of the mind and emotions in his soul. The sin of jealousy within his soul could have made him temporarily "lose his mind," so to speak. He was not thinking right when he killed Abel. He did not think of the possible consequences because his mind was separated from his emotions. He made a decision based on the emotions of the moment, spurred on by the sin of jealousy.

When we sin because of a temporary break in our soul, the sin makes the break more permanent. As a result, we now have to deal with the emotional consequences of sin. After Cain killed Abel, he had to deal with guilt, shame, fear, and a host of other new emotions. He more than likely tried to justify his actions in his mind. To do that, he had to try to shut off what was going on with his emotions. When your emotions are telling you that you are wrong and your mind is trying to say you are right, a break is inevitable. Within Cain's heart, his mind, will, and emotions became separated on a permanent basis.

Whether we are Christians or not, our spirit has a conscience sensitive to right and wrong. When we violate our conscience or when someone else's actions violate us, we feel it in our emotions. Like Cain we feel guilt, shame, fear, or a number of other emotions. When we are violated by someone we trust, we often will try to make sense of their action or behavior with our minds. We almost always justify our own wrong actions. However, the emotional pain of guilt does not necessarily go away.

The emotional pain of guilt and the process of justification cannot operate together. In order to shut off the emotional turmoil and maintain sanity, we have to break a piece of our emotions away from our minds. Though we may no longer think about these things, the emotions of guilt, shame, and fear do not completely go away. They reside in our bodies. They function in our brain's neuro-chemical system, and in our hormonal system, releasing poisons into our body.

How hearts are broken

The Bible speaks of several things that can cause either a bruise or break in our heart or soul. If hearts are bruised repeatedly, a break usually will occur. "But whoso committeth adultery with a woman lacketh understanding: he that doeth it destroyeth his own soul. A wound and dishonor shall he get; and his reproach shall not be wiped away" (Proverbs 6:32-33). The woundedness does not just occur when sexual sin is done voluntarily. One of the most severe breaks is caused by sexual abuse, which can take the form of incest, molestation, or rape. Victoria Johnson's book, *Restoring Broken Vessels: Confronting the Attack on Female Sexuality*, mentioned in chapter two, covers those topics, as well as other sexual issues that all females have to deal with at one time or another. I strongly encourage you to read this book.

God can provide total healing for the damage done in the sexual arena. But when these things are swept under the rug and not dealt with, it will hinder us from moving on up in the Spirit. In fact, much of our involvement in church activities (religion) is often part of the cover-up. We subconsciously think it will erase the feelings of guilt.

In my journey to Spirit living, I've also had to overcome this obstacle. From the time I was five years old until I was twelve, Satan directed sexual misuse and abuse on my life. Those years seriously damaged my soul. I had seen the result of a broken heart in my life, but I did not know why I continued to struggle with fear, worry, guilt, low self-esteem, trust, and discouragement. My biggest struggles as a Christian were probably rooted in that sexual attack on my young self. Thank God for His mercy, grace, and healing in my life.

Tamar, one of David's daughters, is an example of someone in Scripture who had a broken heart. After she was raped by her brother, Amnon "Tamar put ashes on her head, and rent her garment of divers colors that was on her, and laid her hand on her head, and went on crying" (2 Samuel 13:19). Tamar's life was never the same. "She remained desolate in her brother's house" (2 Samuel 13:20). We can see the same thing in the life of Samson. He had been consecrated to serve God, but after visiting prostitutes and being led astray by Delilah, his life was a far cry from his intended purpose.

Sexual sin is not the only cause for breaks in our heart. Idolatry, shame, reproach, and poverty are some of the other things that can cause either bruises or breaks in our soul or heart.

The picture on page 72 shows a broken heart in one of the most severe states of brokenness—one in which there is a separation between the mind, will, and emotions. The break can occur between the mind and emotions, or between the will and emotions, or between the mind and the will. No matter where or to what extent the separation, any break will affect one's behavior.

Without God's Spirit, what we do is determined by the thoughts, feelings, and desires of our soul. There are times when we want to do right, but we find ourselves doing just the opposite of what we want to do. Somehow, our feelings or reasoning abilities do not cooperate with our desires.

> I do not understand what I do. For what I want to do I do not do, but what I hate I do. And if I do what I do not want to do, I agree that the law is good. As it is, it is no longer I myself who do it, but it is sin living in me. I know that nothing good lives in me, that is, in my sinful nature. For I have the desire to do what is good, but I cannot carry it out. For what I do is not the good I want to do; no, the evil I do not want to do—this I keep on doing. (Romans 7: 15-19, NIV)

A double-minded man is unstable in all his ways (James 1:8). The verses above show this instability in Paul. When the heart is divided, you have two minds. One mind is the mind of the human spirit and one mind is the mind of the flesh. God desires us to be single-minded in following Him. This is not possible when our hearts are broken. That's what I discovered with my own broken heart. I wanted to please God, but often behaved in ways that were not pleasing to Him.

Other results of a broken heart

A broken heart can cause a lot of trouble. It causes problems in all parts of the human being—soul, spirit, and body. It affects our body's health by causing dry bones (Proverbs 17:22). Since the bone marrow produces blood and blood is essential to health, dry bones would weaken the ability of the body to fight disease. A broken heart also can cause helplessness and despair (Proverbs 18:14).

A person who is unable to rule over her own spirit is like a city that has its protective walls torn down (Proverbs 25:28). She essentially has no rule over her spirit. Without walls or boundaries, there is no protection. Enemies can get in and out at will, as illustrated below. Because there is no protection from the enemy, a person with a broken heart is vulnerable to many different thieves.

Other evidences of this broken-heartedness may include low self-esteem, guilt, emotional detachment, insecurity, lack of motivation, inability to make wise choices, depression, poor health, anxiety, inability to trust, bitterness, fear, or uncontrolled anger.

Unfortunately, a broken heart opens access to the real enemy of Christians. The person with a broken heart that has not been healed is similar to a house in a crime-infested area that has open windows and doors. The enemy is easily able to get in.

With the enemy coming in and out to kill, steal, and destroy the victory, destiny, and purposes of God, the broken-hearted Christian cannot reflect the nature of her true heavenly Father. The God-given peace, joy, and ability to live right can seep out, leaving the heart vulnerable to worry, anxiety, depression, and the inability to make good decisions. This, unfortunately, reflects the state of many Christian women.

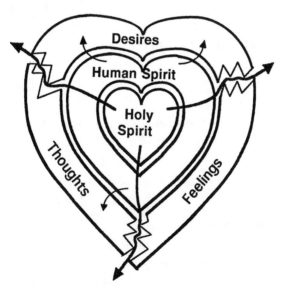

The broken heart and addiction

A person with a broken heart lives in the flesh, demonstrating instability and double-mindedness. A Christian with a broken heart is likely to be carnal. A person with a broken heart is out of control in many ways.

A person with a broken heart may be addicted to drugs, alcohol, food, religion, power, ministry, control, work, or any of a number of things that bring our lives out of balance. In *The Addictive Personality,* Craig Nakken gives this definition of the nature of addictions: "the out of control and aimless searching for wholeness, happiness, and peace through a relationship with an object or event." [1]

The way out of the addictive nature of a broken heart is to experience the wholeness provided by the Holy Spirit. For the Christian, the Holy Spirit has been placed within our human spirits to bring wholeness. Through the process of growth, the soul is weaned from other anchors. When our souls find rest in God, the aimless searching for contentment ceases. "Surely I have calmed and quieted my soul, like a weaned child with his mother; like a weaned child is my soul within me [ceased from fretting]" (Psalm 131:2, Amplified).

Broken hearts are the essence of a Christianity that has a form of godliness, but denies the power thereof (2 Timothy 3:5). Our churches are filled with women with broken hearts. Because of broken hearts, women are not able to demonstrate the Spirit living that brings change. We are unable to fulfill our destiny.

Is there any hope?

There is an answer. It is of utmost importance for us to pursue Spirit life. The pursuit of Spirit living will bring healing to our broken hearts. Pursuing a walk in the Spirit will take us out of religion to a relationship with God that will be dynamic, vital, and glorious (Ephesians 5:18).

The enemy cannot touch a Christian who is living in the Spirit. That's why it is so essential for us to learn to walk in the Spirit. The Holy Spirit of God is all the protection we need. He provides a wall around our lives to prevent the enemy from coming in and out. When we live in the Spirit, it is like living in a house with body guards posted around locked windows and doors. The enemy can't get in. The peace of God guards our mind.

The enemy's only recourse is to devise a plan to keep us from living in the Spirit. He will set up situations that will tempt us to send the Body Guard to the spare room while we take care of things ourselves. Once the Body Guard has been unemployed, because we have either grieved Him by sin or quenched Him by neglect, the enemy can easily break the windows and come in.

Spirit living is not impossible, but it does not come about just because we are Christians. Broken hearts have a major role in keeping us from Spirit living. Broken hearts also result in other heart conditions that hinder Spirit living. We briefly mentioned the addictive nature of broken hearts. The next chapter takes a more detailed look at how addictions or attachments hinder our ability to move on up to Spirit living.

Prayer:
Search me, Oh God, and know my heart; Try me and know my thoughts. See if there be any wicked way in me and lead me to the way everlasting (Psalm 139:23). Lord, show me if I have brokenness in my heart. If I do, please make me whole again.

CHAPTER 7

Attached Hearts Weigh Us Down

"Little children, keep yourselves from idols. Amen."

1 John 5:21

PEOPLE WITH BROKEN HEARTS often seek substitutes for God. The pieces of our hearts attach to other things as a means of trying to find stability. For instance, we may try to find comfort in what we eat. We may try to find purpose in clothes, possessions, or activity. We may substitute television or romance novels for fulfillment in life. These attachments are all substitutes for who God is to be in our lives.

Most of us think of idols as man-made wooden, clay, brass, or other material images used for religious worship in distant lands. While we commend ourselves for never bowing down to a man-made image of God, we do not realize that our broken hearts are full of idolatry. All of the possible heart attachments mentioned above are forms of idolatry. In his book, *Keep Yourself From Idols*, David Alsobrook says, "Any person, thing, attitude, endeavor, concept, doctrine, or any other possible object of affection can easily become an idol!" [1]

Os Guinness and John Seel in their book, *No God But God*, identify the understanding of idolatry as "one of the most powerful spiritual and intellectual concepts in the believer's arsenal." They define idols as follows:

> In the biblical view, anything created—anything at all that is less than God, and most especially the gifts of God—can become idolatrous if it is relied upon inordinately until it becomes a full-blown substitute for God and, thus, an idol. The first duty of believers is to say yes to God; the second is to say no to idols. [2]

Judson Cornwall says something similar, with a different slant. Because of the serious nature of idolatry and our limited understanding of it, at the risk of overstating the point, I'll include his definition from *Things We Adore*.

> Idolatry is principally the response of personal adoration toward something less than Jehovah God, whether that something is self, an object made by ourselves, or a concept we may have embraced. An idol may be metal or mental, carved by man or conceived in the mind; but its outer form is less important than the force it exerts upon our lives. An idol is anything or anyone, including ourselves, that is given the credit for the abilities that only God possesses.[3]

We have already established in the previous chapter that a broken heart is a heart that has the soul separated from the spirit and/or has the parts of the soul separated from each other. When the pieces of our heart are out there, it seems almost as if our heart reaches out to anything to try to glue it back together. Our heart not only tries to find something to hold it together, it also tries to find an anchor to keep it from aimless drifting.

When the separated pieces of our hearts anchor into many different things, we cannot serve God with our all because we have substituted other things for Him. We are actually serving idols. This is a serious condition in violation of the first commandment and of God's lordship in our lives. We have set up idols in our heart. Idols are not just man-made images.

> And the word of the Lord came to me saying, "Son of man, these men have set up their idols in their hearts, and have put right before their faces the stumbling block of their iniquity. Should I be consulted by them at all? Therefore speak to them and tell them, Thus says the Lord God, 'Any man of the house of Israel who sets up his idols in his heart, puts right before his face the

stumbling block of his iniquity, and then comes to the prophet, I the Lord will be brought to give him an answer in the matter in view of the multitude of his idols, in order to lay hold of the hearts of the house of Israel who are estranged from Me through all their idols.' There say to the house of Israel, Thus says the Lord God, 'Repent and turn away from your idols, and turn your faces away from all your abominations.' " (Ezekiel 14:2-6)

God showed me my idols

I mentioned in the last chapter that the discovery of my broken heart led me to see that I was not completely obeying God when I thought I was. Was my heart attached to idols as well? Yes! God slowly began to expose those things in my heart that had taken His place and hindered my obedience to Him.

One stronghold in my thought pattern that had made me hesitant to obey God was the root of fear. This root of fear exhibited itself in fear of what others would think. What was the heart idol behind this root of fear? My heart valued my reputation. It mattered a lot to me that people think well of me.

God has worked with me on this area over and over again. It is always precipitated by a crisis. For instance, once some people were spreading false rumors about me. That was a crisis for me because of my heart's attachment to reputation. I got into gear to try to make them stop. I experienced much anxiety and worry over this issue. I wanted to be God and control their tongue and also the ears of those who received this misinformation.

The first time the Lord exposed this flaw in my heart, He made it clear that I couldn't be His servant if I were preoccupied with trying to please others. I took to heart what God was saying to me. I turned my reputation over to Him, letting go of my need to be responsible for it. The people did not stop saying untrue things about me, but I had my peace back. I didn't let it worry me like before.

Case closed? Not quite. A few years later, it happened again. When we let the bookselling ministry go, the issue of "what will people say?" came up again. That surprised me. I thought it was a dead issue. But this helped me learn that God is always willing and ready to go deeper so that we can go higher. We must never be satisfied. Whenever I sense God calling me higher, I now can expect He will go deeper in this area of fear as well as other strongholds of my flesh—worry, pride, self-righteousness, etc. (You didn't think I was going to name them all, did you?)

My heart attachment to a good reputation has always been a weakness of mine. Even recently, I had to deal with fear of what others would think. Because God continues to work in this area, it's not as serious as it has been. But it doesn't surprise me any more when I realize God is still working on this area. I want Him to do all He needs to do.

The grabbing heart

The nature of a broken heart is that it can easily become attached to things other than God. The broken heart will substitute a variety of things for what God wants to be in our life. I did not understand that sometimes we have to deal with areas in which we thought we had little trouble. For instance, I never would have guessed that I could so easily become attached to food as a substitute for God. But the heart is deceitful and desperately wicked. Who can know it? (Jeremiah 17:9). I did not know my own heart.

We lived in Chicago and I had grown to love the city. I had really good friends there and I felt there were many God-given opportunities for ministry. When my husband began to entertain thoughts of accepting a job offer in Michigan, I knew just what to do. I went straight to the Lord and asked Him to straighten out my husband.

Well, God didn't answer that prayer the way I dictated the answer to Him. I've learned since that prayer is not about us dictating what we want to God. In fact, God made it clear to me that He was behind the potential move. Things were not going the way I wanted them to go. I hoped I could at least get pity from my friends—but that didn't work either.

So, subconsciously I turned to food for solace. I gained twenty pounds in three months. It was then that the Lord showed me that I had substituted food as the source of comfort that He alone could be (2 Corinthians 1: 3-10). I wished He had not waited to show me this until I had gained twenty pounds. It was easy putting the weight on, but I still struggle with getting it off and keeping it off.

Food became an addiction for me when I rebelled against God's plans for my life. God was there to meet my needs, but I refused His help. Thus I was susceptible to becoming attached to something I had never struggled with prior to that time. Craig Nakken explains this in *The Addictive Personality*:

> The addict develops a relationship with an object, hoping to get his or her needs met. This is the insanity of addiction, for people normally get emotional and intimacy needs met through intimate connections with other people, themselves, their community, and with a spiritual power greater than themselves.[4]

Idolatry and the favor of God

Over and over in Scripture, the one condition given for God's favor is to serve and obey Him and Him only. Frequently, we are told that the consequences of failing to do this are removal from God's favor and vulnerability to curses (Deuteronomy 28:14). According to 1 Corinthians 10:14-22, a demon is behind every idol. When our hearts are attached to anything but God, that attachment becomes the tool our enemy can use to control us. When Satan manipulates us because of our attachments, God cannot be in control of our lives. We are like puppets on a string, manipulated by whatever we seek that is not God. If we serve other gods, we remove ourselves from the only One able to solve the problems of our families and communities.

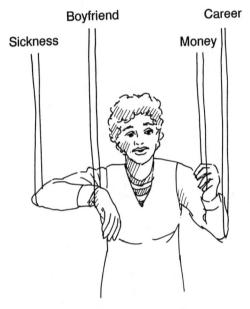

Boyfriend   Career

Sickness   Money

What about God's people? God told His people that He would leave His house to be plundered by the enemy if they turned from Him to serve other gods (2 Chronicles 7:16-21). As God's people, we cry out to Him and wonder why He seems so far away. When God's people try to mix the worship of other gods with the one true God, they start down an ever-widening path of separation and destruction without even knowing it.

Judson Cornwall, in *Things We Adore*, makes the point that the Israelites never voted to replace Jehovah with Baal, they just began to add the gods of the people around them to their own God. This mixing of gods, as Judson puts it, will "subsequently divert, dese-crate and diminish the authority of Jehovah in our lives."[5]

There are many devastating consequences to idolatry:

- We invoke the judgment of God upon our children.

- We become conformed to the image of the gods we worship.

- We become controlled by the devils behind the idols.

- We are without God's protection and help in the battles of life.

It is imperative that we put away the strange gods from among us (Genesis 35:2). This is especially critical if we want to go to Bethel, the house of God, and commune with Him, asking Him to intervene in our problems.

Is God the center of your life?

It is essential that God become the center of our lives. Everything we need can be found in Him. He may use earthly things to provide for our basic needs, but we need not be dependent upon those things. We need only to acknowledge them as the result of God's gracious provision. I am learning the necessity of holding the good things God gives me with an open hand. That will keep my heart pure before God.

God alone is the source of everything. He may give us a job to provide financial resources, but God Himself is our real resource. We thank God for the job, but if the job is gone, we are not devastated because it was just a tool God used to provide for our financial needs. Because we look to God only for fulfillment, we wait on Him to either provide another job or provide for our financial needs another way.

Many single women desire to be married. (Paradoxically, many married women desire to be single!) Whether single or married, we cannot look to a man to be our all in all. The married woman should thank God for her husband, but should not put her husband in the place of God. The single woman may desire a husband, but must not get to the point where she *has* to have a husband. The only thing we *have* to have is Jesus. Jesus is the One we can never do without.

> "One thing have I desired of the Lord, that will I seek after; that I may dwell in the house of the Lord all the days of my life, to behold the beauty of the Lord, and to inquire in his temple" (Psalm 27:4).

When we allow things to control us, we have really put ourselves on the throne of our lives. People with a broken or attached hearts make decisions based in the realm of the soul. They behave according to what they think, feel, or want, which is not necessarily according to the Holy Spirit's working in their human spirit. Self is one of the major idols.

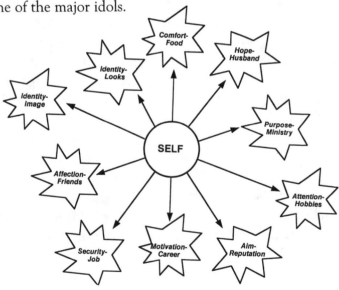

The end result of placing the god of self in the center of our lives is self-deception. The book by Guinness and Seel make this clear in *No God But God*:

> . . . idols will inevitably involve self-centeredness, self-inflation, and self-deception. Idolatry begins with the counterfeiting of God, because only with a counterfeit of God can people remain the center of their lives and loyalties, autonomous architects of their futures. Something within creation will then be idolatrously inflated to fill the God-shaped hole in the individual's world. But a counterfeit is a lie, not the real thing. It must present itself through self-deception, often with images suggesting that the idol will fulfill promises for the good life.[6]

Throwing down idols

The process of detaching from our attachments is very painful. However, it is a necessary part of learning to be people of the Spirit. I mentioned the five years of trials in my own life. That was part of God's grace upon my life to free me to be wholly His. I did not fully understand what God was doing and was very frustrated. Unfortunately, the pain of this process causes many people to turn back from pursuing the things of the Spirit.

It is so very important to submit to the painful process of detachment if we want to move from religion to authentic Christianity. Our attachments are sometimes part of our religion. We use meetings and church as a means to find security and comfort. Religion has become a substitute for God Himself. That may seem contradictory, but it is possible that "religion" was not a true relationship with God in the first place.

It is easy for religion to become a substitute for God when the power behind that religion is not the power of God. To move into authentic Christianity and Spirit living, all religious props must be removed. To truly remove the cancerous tumor from the healthy tissue takes a highly skilled surgeon. Thank God, it can be done.

The Lord has shown me that I have often tried to fix my broken heart by my attachments. I have substituted my family, my friends, or my intellectual ability for the source of wisdom, esteem, or hope in life.

I already shared that I have used food for comfort. God convicted me of using ministry as my source of purpose. God was not pleased. He had to break the attachments so that I could be anchored in Him alone. My heart has looked like this illustration:

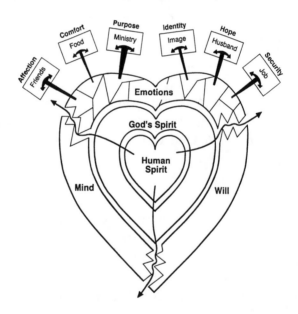

As we learn to live in the Spirit, God will root out all that has taken the place of Christ in our lives. God will re-anchor us in Himself. For the kingdom of God to prevail, God has to reign as its King.

God wants my heart to be fully anchored in Him, so that He alone controls me and the things around me that I get attached to so easily. When I give everything that I am accustomed to pursuing or finding value in over to Him, the power those things have to control me is gone. A heart fully anchored in God looks like this next illustration:

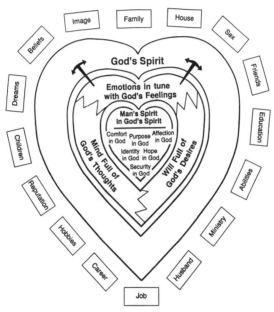

Many times we are attached to something and do not even know it until the object or person threatens to be removed from our lives. Our attachments can hold us back from soaring in the life of the Spirit. God has to remove us from our attachments or remove our attachments from us. When our hearts are anchored in anything but God, that anchor has to be severed if we want to continue growing in the things of the Spirit. "Let us put away the weights of sin that so easily beset us." (Hebrews 12:3)

Prayer:

God, I have been guilty of setting up idols in my heart. My heart has been deceitful and wicked. I don't know my own heart. Wash my heart by the water of Your Word. I give you permission to remove the false anchors of my heart so that I might live in the Spirit.

CHAPTER 8

Mouth Traps and Anger

". . . Lest any root of bitterness springing up trouble you."
Hebrews 12:15

THERE IS A STRONG CONNECTION between God's purpose for women and our use of words. With women's abilities to bring life, nurturing, and encouragement through communication, there is nothing we cannot do if we put our minds and tongues to it.

Satan fully knows the power women have as communicators. The power of communication is strong. Communication is what God had to stop when people were trying to build the tower of Babel.

God wants us to use our ability to communicate to build a communication tower to heaven, but Satan is bent on destroying it. Satan is behind all of the injustices against women because he wants to keep us away from our God-given tasks. Satan has conspired to keep us fighting the wrong battles.

A conspiracy is a secret plan to accomplish an evil end. There is a conspiracy against women. The well-planned strategy is spiritual. It was cooked up in hell by the enemy of God. The purpose of the conspiracy is to remove us from God's favor and to keep us from fulfilling our God-given destiny. We have already examined one aspect of this conspiracy: broken hearts and attached hearts.

Bitter roots

In order to live in the Spirit, each of us has to deal with bitterness. Bitterness can occur naturally when we are wronged or treated with injustice. That's been the continuing plight of African Americans.

Unfortunately, that bitterness has left a tree in many African American communities which bears undesirable fruit.

What is the undesirable fruit? Violence, conflicts, marital discord, drugs, teen pregnancies, divorce, disease, immorality, unhappiness, suicide, incarcerations, anxiety, worry, fear, gossip, and slander—to name a few. By mentioning this fruit, we do not mean to detract from the good fruit in African American communities—such as hard work, generosity, ingenuity, education, kindness, family togetherness, etc. But we need to deal with the rotten fruit because it will eventually spoil the good fruit.

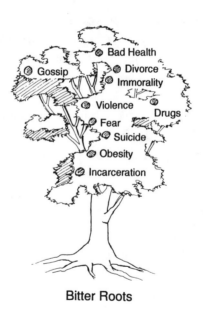

Bitter Roots

Dealing with rotten fruit

What do you do if you don't want bad fruit? You can always try plucking all the fruit from the tree and discarding it. That might work for a season, but when the next fruit-bearing season comes, you'll just have more bad fruit to pick.

We have to understand something about fruit: it grows on trees, which originate from roots (Isaiah 37:31). We need to examine the fruit in our lives. Is it good or bad? Did it come from a good tree or an evil tree? Is the fruit from Christian homes different from that of non-Christian homes? Statistics tell us that the degree of divorce, teen sexual activity, and drug use is about the same in the homes of those who go to church as in those who don't. The bad fruit we see today grows from a bitter root, indeed.

> Follow peace with all men, and holiness, without which no man shall see the Lord: Looking diligently lest any man fail of the grace of God; lest any root of bitterness springing up trouble you, and thereby many be defiled. (Hebrews 12:14-15)

The definition of *root* is origin, cause, or source. Bitterness is the origin, cause, and source of the problems in America's cities. Bitterness first causes problems for individuals. Then it spreads to whole families and communities.

Webster's Collegiate Dictionary, Tenth Edition defines *bitter* as "intense animosity (enemies); harshly reproachful (complaints); cynicism and rancor (contempt); intensely unpleasant, especially in coldness or rawness; expressive of severe pain, grief, or regret."

Vine's Expository Dictionary of Biblical Words says *bitter* is taken from a root meaning "to cut, to prick," hence, "pointed, sharp, keen."

The Complete Word Study Dictionary: New Testament: In the Old Testament, "it (bitter) is used to indicate the fruits of the wild vine or bitter gourd which are so excessively bitter and acrid as to be a kind of poison. In the New Testament, used of taste, meaning bitter, acrid, brackish (James 3:11). Metaphorically it means bitter, cruel, malignant (James 3:14, indicating bitter, harsh, cruel feeling)."

Pain and grief give root to bitterness. When the bitterness springs up in our lives, we cannot love others. "Springing" means to generate, produce, bring forth, let grow according to *The Complete Word Study Dictionary*. Bitterness in our hearts produces jealousy, self-centeredness, envy, and self-seeking or untrusting behavior.

Bitterness is also expressed in our speech. Bitterness defiles our tongues. Defiled tongues defile others. We have already seen the connection between our hearts and tongue. The enemy adds bitter roots to broken hearts to make sure he steals the power and purpose of the gift of communication that God has given women. It's a mouth trap. Satan has to foul up our communication skills in order to put a stop to what God would have us build.

The connection between bitterness and our speech is found in the following verses:

> Their throat is an open sepulcher; with their tongues they have used deceit; the poison of asps is under their lips: whose mouth is full of cursing and bitterness. (Romans 3:13-14)

> Let all bitterness, and wrath, and anger and clamor, and evil speaking, be put away from you, with all malice. (Ephesians 4:31)

Our words are very important. "But I say unto you, that every idle word that men shall speak, they shall give account thereof in the day of judgment. For by thy words thou shalt be justified, and by thy words thou shalt be condemned." (Matthew 12:36-37)

Serving God stands on the two commandments: (1) Love God with all of your heart, soul, mind, and strength, and (2) Love your neighbor as yourself. When our hearts are broken and attached, we can't love God with our whole heart. When our tongues are defiled, Satan then is able to get us to neglect the second commandment. You cannot love your neighbor if your tongue is not tamed.

A defiled tongue is the result of a broken heart and bitter roots. It is Satan's ultimate goal for the pain he brings into our lives. If he can get our tongues, he has *us*! He can then manipulate the very instrument that God has given us to bring life to others to suit his evil purposes.

Satan has his spiritual equation.

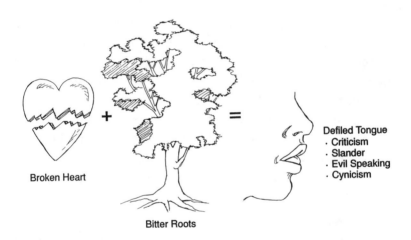

Broken Heart

Bitter Roots

Defiled Tongue
· Criticism
· Slander
· Evil Speaking
· Cynicism

Broken hearts + bitter roots = defiled tongues.

The root of bitterness will affect what flows from our tongues. If our tongues speak unpleasantness, animosity, cynicism, contempt, coldness, or rawness, we have a bitter root. Death also can flow out of the tongue (Proverbs 18:21). A defiled tongue brings death, not life.

We have talked a lot about the tongue, because I believe the improper use of our tongues is one of the biggest reasons we grieve the Holy Spirit. If we grieve the Holy Spirit, we cannot continue in things of the Spirit.

> Let no corrupt communication proceed out of your mouth, but that which is good to the use of edifying, that it may minister grace unto the hearers. And grieve not the Holy Spirit of God, whereby ye are sealed unto the day or redemption. (Ephesians 4:29-30)

Satan has always been after the seed of women. Satan's purposes now are to get a hook into our tongues so that we destroy our seed (our young) with acts such as criticisms, belittling, outbursts of anger, or prayerlessness. If he cannot get us in this manner, he will get us to be so tired and depressed that we are of little help to our seed. God wants to move us on up in the Spirit so that our words are full of faith, Spirit-filled, and life producing.

God can lay an ax to the root of bitterness, destroying the fruit of complaining, harshness, animosity, coldness, and all the other negative characteristics. God wants to replace these with the fruit of the Spirit: love, joy, peace, patience, kindness, goodness, faithfulness, gentleness, and self-control.

Taking an ax to the root

Anger is a legitimate emotion that is expressed when wrong or injustice is done, or when something is not right. It is not right to be belittled, abused, controlled, or taken advantage of in any way. Women treated in unkind ways often experience tremendous anger. Dr. Les Carter in *The Anger Workbook* says anger has "an intent to preserve (1) personal worth, (2) essential needs, and (3) basic convictions."[1]

Understanding is key to taking an ax to the root of bitterness. because anger precedes bitterness, it is important to know how to handle anger and how to act when we are angry.

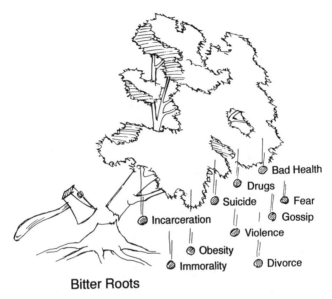

Bitter Roots

Dr. Dwight Carlson, author of *Overcoming Hurts and Anger*, defines anger as "an automatic reaction to any real or imagined insult, frustration, or injustice, producing emotional agitation, which the person may or may not be aware of, but which will seek expression in some sort of aggressive, defensive, or destructive manner to oneself or others." [2]

It's okay to be angry, but the Bible says, "Be angry and sin not" (Ephesians 4:26). How do we not sin when we are angry?

To answer that question, let's consider the opposite: how *do* we sin when we are angry? Most of the time we sin by the wrong use of our tongue. The Lord convicted me that when I was angry with the situation on my job, at my husband, myself, or just life in general, I often took it out on my children by yelling at them. You would never hear me do it. If you came to my door, I could be ever so kind and sweet you would never believe that I ever yelled at my children. But God knew. He began to show me that walking in the Spirit with His agape love—patience, kindness, forbearance, hope—was for my children, too! The nature of the job of raising children gives us many opportunities to come to the end of our own ropes and practice God's agape love. Don't worry if you don't have children of your own; a racist boss, ornery neighbor, difficult mother-in-law, or jealous friend can all qualify us for lessons in agape love. Other wrong uses of our tongue that we pour out on others include slander, criticisms, sarcasm, and harsh words.

Another way I have sinned when angry is to turn anger inward. Anger turned inward often becomes depression in women. I have a tendency to be down or discouraged when things don't go my way or I don't understand what is going on in my life. Of course, God is sovereign and can make everything work together for good (Romans 8:28). When I allow circumstances to discourage me, I cease letting God be God and try to get myself back on the throne.

Discouragement can lead to despair or depression. That has happened to me, more than once. When we lived in Nigeria with our two children and were already planning to return to the States, I definitely knew that was the one time in my marriage I did not want to get pregnant. In spite of all my planning, I still got pregnant (with my third child). This pregnancy gave me great cause to worry. I became depressed. We would be without insurance when the child was due. I could just see the bills piling up. I knew we would have to beg money from family and friends or become a charity case. I wasted a lot of time being depressed and worried for nothing. To make a long story short, I ended up having to pay $3 out of my pocket when it was all over. Trying to play God is really no fun at all, and is senseless because He takes such good care of us.

Another way we use anger the wrong way is to turn from God when we do not understand what is happening in our lives. When things happen to us over which we have no control, it is easy to point at God as the bad guy. If He is supposed to be sovereign and in control, why did He let this happen? For many years, I questioned God about why He did not stop the sexual attack on my life from the ages of five to twelve. Without realizing it, I harbored a lot of bitterness and resentment toward God. Even though I was religious, I really was a backsliding church worker and church pew occupant. I had to admit the anger with God and allow God to work through it all before I received my healing. We can't be used of God fully against Satan if we have unresolved bitterness toward God.

The right use of the energy of anger

The emotion of anger is loaded with energy. God wants us to use that energy against Satan. Depending on our personal response to wrong, we have seen how we can use the leftover energy of anger against ourselves, as in depression; against others, as in yelling; and against God, as in backsliding. From our definitions of anger, anger gives us energy to protect ourselves and others. After we have protected ourselves, we still probably will have some anger left over. That un-spent anger can give us energy for the purposes of hurt, retaliation, revenge or it can be used to make a difference in this evil world.

We could use the energy of anger against the Devil, by walking in the Spirit and loving our enemies. For whom or what do you use your anger? I urge you to use the energy of anger for God—and against the Devil.

Let's suppose each of us has one hundred points of anger to use in our lifetime. If we use all 100 points of anger against people or situations we have no control over, how many points of anger do we have left to fight the real enemy of our souls?

God is looking for women who will stop being angry at the tools Satan has used and develop a righteous indignation against

Satan himself. Yes, God is sovereign. God is in control. But this earth is not heaven. There is an evil presence here that is behind all the evil that goes on. Because God is sovereign, He is able to make good use of bad things. God recycles trash. What Satan means for evil, God can mean for good to bring to pass the salvation of many people (Genesis 50:20). We may not understand everything, but I challenge you to use each occasion for anger as an opportunity to come closer to God and to pray for the person who is being used by Satan.

Other traps of anger

As a result of our anger, we try unduly to control others. Barbara Cook speaks of this trap in her excellent book, *The Control Trap*. If we want God in complete control of our lives, however, we have to surrender the lives of the people we love into His hands. It is very difficult to let God take care of the son or daughter who is on drugs, the demanding boss, the unkind mother-in-law, or wavering husband. But we have to give these people into the hands of God. God can do a much better job of controlling and changing them than you or I can.

When we take matters into our own hands, we often try to cause change by manipulation, intimidation, threats, or domination. When we do this, we are trusting in the arm of the flesh and are rebelling against God. We cannot be blessed when we trust in the arm of the flesh. That is rebellion, which is as the sin of witchcraft (1 Samuel 15:23).

Man-made control is forcing others to do what we think they should do. When we try to control people, we are really taking the place of God in their lives. Even God gives people freedom of choice! When we take things into our own hands and try to change people by manipulation, threats, domination, or other ways of the flesh, we show that we do not depend entirely on God.

Many of us are not satisfied until everything around us is under our control. We want to control the way others spend their time and what they do or do not do. We even want to control the way others perceive us. Just recently, the Lord showed me how I was scheming to try to control what a friend would think about something I was doing. The Lord reminded me that was not my job. I am not God. Perhaps God wanted to deal with her and I was trying to protect her from His work in her life.

Many times, when we are out of control internally because of our broken hearts, we spend all our energy trying to control everything around us. The solution is to acknowledge our commitment to God and recognize His ability to bring the situations around us under control. Then we will no longer have the need to control everybody and everything else. Some of you may be able to identify someone you know, perhaps yourself, with the fictitious person described below.

Mary has three grown children. She is very likable, but she is always in everybody's business. Whenever you are in a conversation with another person and Mary is around, she'll butt in and give her two cents worth. Of course, you never asked her opinion. She always has some unsolicited advice for you. Her children are tired of her running their lives. Two have moved out of town to get away from her. Her husband has learned to ignore her. He stays away from home as much as possible. Mary is a "control freak," but she doesn't know it.

Freedom is releasing others to do as they choose. It is recognizing that other people have the right to make choices and allowing them to use that God-given right. It is exercising our power with God—instead of using control over people—to initiate change.

The way of the Spirit

The ways of the Spirit are the ways of God, far above our ways. Going God's way, we exchange ungodly anger for godly energy, enabling us to fight our real enemy. We use the energy of anger as the impetus to push us to change.

When we do not properly understand how to be angry and yet not sin, we continue to use our tongues unwisely. When we don't properly use the energy of anger, we bring evil—not only upon ourselves but upon our families, churches, and others—by our murmuring, complaining, and speaking negative words.

I see a great army of women, directing all the energy of their anger against Satan. What a marvelous thing that will be! Wounded women with broken hearts and bitter roots are susceptible to many traps, we can go beyond the traps to be warriors with God in the right battle as we move on up to Spirit living.

Prayer:

God, I want to be a member of your army burning with righteous indignation against Satan. Teach me how to be angry and not sin. Forgive me for trying to control everything instead of giving that right to You. Merciful, Father, thank You for Your love, kindness, faithfulness, and pursuit of me when I have been so far from You and Your ways. Let the words of my mouth and meditation of my heart be acceptable in your sight. Put a watch over the door of my mouth. Thank you for your ability to tame my tongue. I ask you to order my tongue by your Word.

SECTION III

Movin' On Up to Spirit Living

CHAPTER 9

Life in God's Spirit

"For the law of the Spirit of life in Christ Jesus hath
made me free from the law of sin and death."

Romans 8:2

THE DEVELOPMENT OF THE Spirit in us brings the maturing of our character. The development of our walk in the Spirit
is evidenced by our level of service to others. As we learn to move
deeper into the waters of the Spirit, we will develop in power. The
person who emphasizes the development of love and refuses to
develop in power will only experience frustration at her inability
to help others. The Spirit of God within is not content until He is
able to reach out to others in service. It is essential to rely on God
for the abilities or gifts that come only from Him if you really want
to bring others out of bondage, heal broken hearts, and bring the
immature into maturity.

By the same token, it is possible to experience greater levels of
power and neglect the walk of love. Sooner or later, power that is
not tempered by love and a servant's attitude will corrupt a person.
It is possible to walk in the power and gifts of God and still be
immature.

Ideally, we should grow in things of the Spirit while allowing
the Holy Spirit within to mature us at the same time. We should
develop simultaneously in love and power. A spiritual person is
measured by both character and ability. It appears we develop
according to what is emphasized by those around us. Most of the
time, the emphasis is on one aspect or the other, but rarely on both.

Bringing it all together

We are to walk in the Spirit, live in the Spirit, be filled with the
Spirit, and be led by the Spirit. Many people use the Spirit of God

like drinking water. When they are thirsty, they think a little sip will do. We are to live in the Spirit like a fish lives in the water. Most of the people of God are more like swimmers than fish. We go to the river and take a swim whenever it is convenient, but we do not live in the river.

God does not want to just be in us; He wants to fill us. He is not content to fill us up with the Spirit of God upon occasion; He desires us to remain full. In order to be people of the Spirit, we also have to be people who are completely immersed in the Spirit. It is important to see the two-fold nature of the operation of the Spirit of God. One dimension is the work of the Spirit within us. This has traditionally been the understanding of the fruit of the Spirit. The other is our walk in Him. This has traditionally been the understanding of the gifts of the Spirit.

There are at least seven operations of the Holy Spirit in our lives. These seven operations cover both of the two-fold dimensions of the work of the Spirit. Most Christians settle for one or two, while some more mature Christians may exhibit as many as three or four of these operations. But the fullness of the stature of Christ in our lives encompasses all seven operations (see list below). It is important that every member of the Body of Christ walk in this fullness.

1. The Spirit of God in us	John 14:17; John 20:22; 2 Cor. 1:22; Ephesians 1:13; Romans 8:9
2. The Spirit of God with us	John 14:16-17
3. The Spirit of God for us	Romans 8:31
4. Spirit of God upon us	Luke 24:49; Acts 1:8; Acts 2:3
5. Spirit of God filling us	Acts 2:4; Ephesians 5:18
6. Spirit of God through us	John 4:14; John 7:38-39; 2 Cor. 4:12
7. Spirit of God about us	Ephesians 4:5; Galatians

1. The Spirit of God in us:

Think of this as water being poured into a cup. Once we have experienced the new birth for our beginning in the spirit realm, we should rely upon God's Spirit for maintenance and sustenance.

To have the Spirit of God within, we have only to turn our lives over to God through Jesus Christ. If you confess with your mouth the Lord Jesus Christ and believe in your heart that God has raised Jesus from the dead, you will be saved (Romans 10:9). We have to accept the death, burial, and resurrection of Jesus as sacrifice for our sins. At the time of the new birth, the Holy Spirit of God takes up residence within the new believer.

2. The Spirit of God with us:

Think of this as a bucket of water at our sides, helpful in time of need. The Holy Spirit is at our sides as our comforter.

From the new birth on, the Holy Spirit is with the believer. He is there as comforter, guide, and teacher; He brings things to our memory. He promises to always be with us. We can call upon Him in need. He comes along beside us (John 14:16-17, 26). The Holy Spirit has been a great comfort to me in recent times of bereavement. He also has used others to bring me comfort.

3. The Spirit of God for us:

Think of this as water power producing electricity for our use. In this operation, the Holy Spirit works for us by protecting us from the enemy. If God be for us, who can be against us? We all need His supernatural help at one time or another.

Paul experienced the Holy Spirit being for him. There were many people against Paul. But the Holy Spirit was for him, warning him about plots against him. The Holy Spirit helped him escape the plans of his enemies (Acts 23:12-23). The Holy Spirit even helped him recover from severe beatings (Acts 14:19-20; 2 Corinthians 11:23).

Today, the Holy Spirit can be for us in our jobs or elsewhere when others plot against us. When we turn to other sources and neglect to turn to God for help, God will not force His help upon us. Many times God allows all other help to dry up so that we are forced to turn to Him.

4. The Spirit of God upon us:

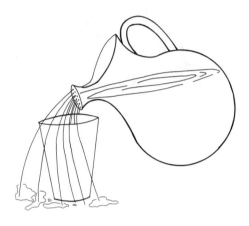

Think of the water from a shower falling on you. This operation is often called "baptism of the Spirit." If it is a one-time event, it dries up. It is meant to provide continual power.

Differences abound among Christians about the baptism of the Holy Spirit. I really believe it is okay for members in the Body of Christ to have different convictions about a variety of things. What one believes about the Baptism of the Holy Spirit is not as important as how one treats others who do not believe the same. Humility, prayer, esteeming others better than ourselves, and recognizing our need for diversity is part of Spirit living.

Some believe the baptism of the Holy Spirit takes place at the new birth, while others believe it takes place later. I personally believe we receive all the Holy Spirit has to give us at the new birth. God has given us everything that pertains to life and godliness through the knowledge of Him (2 Peter 1:3). But the newborn

Christian may not know all that she has received at that time. It's like this; I have a computer that has a lot of things on it which I have not yet discovered. When I make a particular discovery, it's new to me because I had not seen that before, but, it had been there all the time, because it came with the computer when I bought it. If I had been instructed about all that was available when I bought the computer, I would have experienced the full benefits all along. There are a lot of things the Spirit of God has for us that many of us have not yet received instructions on.

5. The Spirit of God filling us:

Think of this as water being poured into you all the way to the brim. In the book of Acts, we see that the Christians were filled again after they prayed (Acts 4:31). Paul instructed the Ephesians to keep on being filled with the Spirit (Ephesians 5:18). We get filled by asking the Holy Spirit to fill us and by emptying ourselves of our own resources.

The Holy Spirit fills us up many times in our lives until we come to a state of being full of the Spirit. That comes as we live in the Spirit. A cup can be filled with water and the water eventually will evaporate. But if the cup full of water is placed at the bottom of the river, the cup will stay full.

6. The Spirit of God through us:

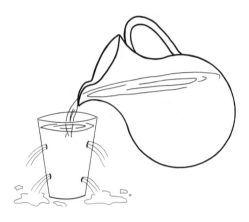

Think of this as water flowing out through your pores to help others. This is the overflow of the Spirit in our lives that touches the lives of others.

The Holy Spirit flows through us to others as we allow Him to use us in ministry to others. We may be used to comfort, to teach, or to use any of the gifts of the Spirit operating through us to help others. When people were used by God to comfort me in recent bereavements, they allowed the Holy Spirit to flow through them.

Most often the Holy Spirit flows through our souls, through our attitude, speech, and behavior expressed to others. But, at times, the Spirit of God can actually flow through our physical bodies when we use our hands in godly touches. The Spirit of God can be ministered to others through the laying on of hands (Acts 3:7; 9:17). As Spirit-filled mothers, this can be a ministry to our children, even to our teens. I'm not a touchy-touchy person by nature, but God has prompted me to make changes in this area. Of course, we have to be wary of so-called therapeutic touches by those who do not necessarily live their lives by the Bible.

7. **The Spirit of God about us:**

Think of this as swimming in a sea. We are surrounded by the Spirit realm, flowing over, under, and around us. In that realm, we make decisions that sow to the spirit instead of to the flesh. This is the culmination of God's work in us and our walk in the Spirit.

Eventually, we move to the place of living in the Spirit. This is the place God wants all of us to come to. This seventh operation of the Spirit is God's ultimate intention for us. It does not just get a little water in us. Think of it as taking in water with every breath we breathe so that we are saturated. This is possible only when we make the ways of the Spirit our lifestyle.

The seventh operation is a coming together of the operation of us in the Spirit and the Spirit in us. As we live in the Spirit, we are continuously full of the Spirit because we do not get away from things of the Spirit long enough for the Spirit to diminish in our lives. Christ is fully formed within us. As the Spirit is all about us, our lives reflect the change God has been orchestrating internally, and we become lights to a dark world. This is living in the Spirit. We have mentioned the possibility of visiting the Spirit and not living there. When we visit the Spirit, we use the water when it is convenient for us, but we hop back out when it is inconvenient. The water evaporates if we are out too long. Living in the Spirit does not allow us to dry up spiritually.

Being full of the Spirit is not an out-of-reach ideology. It is practical Christianity when we choose to act out of love, kindness, forgiveness, and tenderheartedness, praying for those who offend us, blessing those who curse us. As we consistently make those choices we come to the place of living in the Spirit.

God wants us to move on up in the Spirit. We are given daily opportunities to choose to walk in light or to walk in darkness; to walk by the Spirit or to walk by the flesh. We need to know these rules for walking in the light if we want to *stay* in the Spirit. It is possible to learn to walk in the Spirit on a consistent basis and yet still go back to living in the flesh. Don't ever think you will get to a place where you can't be tempted. Yes, we've said Satan can't touch you when you're in the Spirit. But he'll devise a plan to tempt you to come outside and play with him. Don't play with strife, jealousy, pride, bitterness, evil communications, or anything else he offers. It's all a ploy.

In order to get you out from the secret place, Satan has to do something to get you to stop seeking or setting your affections on things above. He does that by getting you to seek something here below—position, possessions, purpose. He'll get you to entertain strife, instead of peace. He'll tempt you to be unthankful. He has many plans. He knows your vulnerable points. The higher you go in the Spirit, the more serious and sophisticated he gets.

I wish I could devise a neat formula that if followed would keep everyone from falling into Satan's traps. Each of us is unique. Even if I found a formula that worked for me, it may not work for you. God does not give formulas. He gives us principles that we should follow. Just do what God says do. It's that simple. Though I cannot list all of His directions to us, I have compiled some of the rules we should follow daily:

- Initial "putting on" (Galatians 3:17)
- Seek things above (Colossians 3:1; Matthew 6:21, 33)
- Set affections on things above (Colossians 3:2)
- Put to death earthly nature (Colossians 3:5, Romans 6:6,11-14)

- Put aside the old ways (Colossians 3:8; Ephesians 4:22)
- Put on the new man (Colossians 3:10; Ephesians 4:24)
- Let God's peace rule (Colossians 3:15 Romans 14:17, 16:20)
- Be thankful (Colossians 3:15, 17)
- Let the Word dwell in you richly (Colossians 3:16)
- Do everything in Jesus' name (Colossians 3:17)

Prayer:

I admit I have settled for less of the work of Your Spirit in me than You have wanted me to. I realize I have a lot to learn about Your ways. Teach me Your ways. I do not want to come up short on anything You have for me. I give all of my fears and hesitations to You. Teach me to fear You more than I fear anyone or anything else. Forgive me for often taking the low road of anger and unforgiveness. It is amazing how You can forgive me so freely, yet I hold on to bitterness towards others. I know You have given me everything that pertains to life and godliness. I cannot excuse myself, neither can I blame anyone else. Let the rules of Your Spirit become part of my daily behavior.

CHAPTER 10

The Walk in the Spirit

"If we live in the Spirit, let us also walk in the Spirit."

Galatians 5:25

IN THIS CHAPTER, WE WILL EXAMINE the work of the Holy Spirit available to the people of God to do the works of Jesus. God enables us to serve others through the abilities He gives us as we learn to walk in Him.

Walking in the Spirit is walking clothed in the armor of God. Putting on armor is like putting on Christ. We are continuously naked before God, but He covers our weaknesses, provides us a shield, and puts a wall of protection between us and the world. In order to be comfortable serving others with the abilities given us by the Spirit of God, we have to be comfortable with walking in the Spirit.

Four levels of walk in the Spirit

Ezekiel tells us of four depths that are available to those who want to walk in the Spirit (47: 1-9). These verses describe four different levels of water. (In Scripture, water often is a symbol of God's Spirit.)

> Then brought he me out of the way of the gate northward, and led me about the way without unto the outer gate by the way that looketh eastward; and, behold there ran out waters on the right side. And when the man that had the line in his hand went forth eastward, he measured a thousand cubits, and he brought me through the waters; the waters were to the ankles. . . .the waters were to the knees. . . . the waters were to the loins. Afterward he measured a thousand; and it was a river that I could not pass over: for the waters were risen, waters to swim in, a river that could not be passed over.

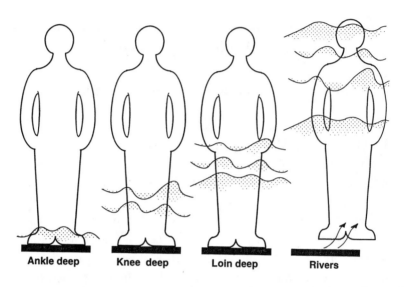

Ankle deep   Knee deep   Loin deep   Rivers

The walk in the Spirit is our development in the gifts and power of God to serve others. We all start out walking in the Spirit at the ankle-deep level. At that level, you are able to see your feet. You are still pretty much in control. The water is there, but you can move about as you please. Many people have experienced ankle-deep service and think they have it made, not realizing they have only begun the walk in the Spirit. The service at this level might encompass praying for or encouraging someone. It could mean giving someone a Scripture verse.

The next level, knee-deep brings us a little deeper in the things of the Spirit. At this point, you might have a little difficulty moving around in the water. You can't move as freely as before. It is harder to see your feet. But they still are on solid ground and you can still decide where you'll go in the water. The list of spiritual gifts listed in Romans 12 is where I see this level of service. An understanding of one's motivational gifts is a foundation to serving others. There is a whole body of information concerning the characteristics, strengths, weakness of those with the gift of giving, serving, teaching, and all the others. A person can easily identify the primary gift they exercise from this list. The term motivational gifts is used when describing this list of gifts because the primary gift a person identifies with motivates all of their life. One helpful book is *Discover Your God-given Gifts* by Don & Katie Fortune.

The Christians who go from ankle-deep to the knee-deep things of God's Spirit often feel they have hit the ultimate in walking with God, going so far as to look down on their brothers and sisters who are only ankle deep in Christ!

Then we have those who go loin-deep in walking in the Spirit. At this level, you are over half-covered with water. It is increasingly more difficult to move around. Your legs are completely underwater. The water hinders, rather than helps your movement. This is the point at which it appears more attractive to turn back to a shallower depth. Staying in the loin-deep water is very uncomfortable. The choice is to advance further and risk drowning in the deep water, or turn around and go back. Many people who make it to loin-deep water turn back. Others think they are in heaven. Little do they know, this place, too, is just a step along the way to where God wants to take them. Here one might be experiencing the gifts of the Spirit listed in 1 Corinthians 12.

The place God wants all of us to be is completely immersed in the Spirit. Our final development in the Spirit is to live like a fish in the river, being carried wherever the river takes us and never coming out. The river (God's Spirit) controls us! This is the deepest and final level. This is the ministry of life that Paul speaks about in 2 Corinthians 4.

> For we have this treasure in earthen vessels, that the excellency of the power may be of God, and not of us. We are troubled on every side, yet not distressed; we are preplexed, but not in

despair; Persecuted, but not forsaken; cast down, but not de stroyed; Always bearing about in the body the dying of the Lord Jesus, that the life also of Jesus might be made manifest in our mortal flesh. So then death worketh in us, but life in you. (1 Corinthians 4:7-12)

It is hard to proceed to the deepest level. We are no longer in control there, and it feels like drowning. It is difficult to get there because we have to die to our own selves. At this level, the Spirit of God truly controls our lives and our service. At that level, the water is over our head and we go where the river takes us. It may take us before kings and queens, or it may take us to the homeless. Where the river takes us does not matter to us. The important thing is that the Spirit of God leads us there.

The gifts of the Spirit

God gives us gifts to enable us to serve others with His power. We should not be ignorant of spiritual gifts (1 Corinthians 12:1). Let's take a look at the two main passages of Scripture that speak of the spiritual gifts God gives to individual members of His Body, Romans 12 and 1 Corinthians 12. The other list of gifts given to the Body as a whole to help us grow up is found in Ephesians 4. We will look briefly at those in Chapter Eighteen.

I believe there is a need for each of us to be open to progress through all four levels of spiritual power, but as I've studied these two passages, I was intrigued by the similarities in the contexts surrounding both passages. I think there is a place to see the gifts of the Spirit in the context of a body and not just in individual members.

My own personal opinion is not that important. But the Bible says we should not be ignorant, and if people are going to be able to move beyond broken hearts, it is important to recognize the power of God available to undo what God's enemy has been able to accomplish. So let's look at the context of the discussion of gifts, and the two lists of gifts. I'll bring up a few thought-provoking questions, but will deliberately restrict my comments because of the sensitive nature of this material to many in the Body of Christ.

The Body as a whole

The following verses immediately follow the list of gifts in 1 Corinthians 12:

> For as the body is one, and hath many members, and all the members of that one body, being many, are one body: so also is Christ. . . . For the body is not one member, but many. . . .If the whole body were an eye, where were the hearing? If the whole were hearing, where were the smelling? But now hath God set the members every one of them in the body, as it hath pleased him. And if they were all one member, where were the body? And now are they many members, yet but one body. (1 Corinthians 12: 12, 14, 17-20)

The passage below precedes the list of gifts in Romans 12:

> For I say, through the grace given unto me, every man that is among you, not to think of himself more highly than he ought to think; but to think soberly, according as God hath dealt to every man the measure of faith. For as we have many members in one body, and all members have not the same office: So we, being many, are one body in Christ, and every one members one of another. (Romans 12:3-5)

It always amazes me that discussion on the gifts of the Spirit can cause so much division, pride, and unloving behavior among members of the Body of Christ, when both of these passages have the common thread of Christians being members of the same body.

Could it be possible that we have looked at gifts too much from the individual perspective, when God meant it to be seen as something He gave us as a Body, no matter who exercises which gifts. Could it be we have used gifts—or the lack of gifts—as a matter of individual pride?

Pursue love

This first passage of Scripture comes after the discussion of gifts listed in 1 Corinthians 12:

> But covet earnestly the best gifts: and yet show I unto you a more excellent way. Though I speak with the tongues of men and of angels, and have not charity, I am become as sounding brass, or a tinkling cymbal. And though I have the gift of prophecy, and understand all mysteries, and all knowledge; and though I have all faith, so that I could remove mountains, and have not charity, I am nothing. And though I bestow all my goods to feed the poor, and though I give my body to be burned, and have not charity, it profiteth me nothing. Charity suffereth long, and is kind; charity envieth not; charity vaunteth not itself, is not puffed up, doth not behave itself unseemly, seeketh not her own, is not easily provoked, thinketh no evil; rejoiceth not in iniquity, but rejoiceth in the truth; beareth all things, believeth all things, hopeth all things, endureth all things. (1 Corinthians 12:31-13:7)

This set of verses follows the list of gifts in Romans 12:

> Let love be without dissimulation. Abhor that which is evil; cleave to that which is good. Be kindly affectioned one to another with brotherly love; in honor preferring one another; . . . Rejoicing in hope; patient in tribulation; continuing instant in prayer; distributing to the necessity of saints; given to hospitality. Bless them which persecute you; bless and curse not. Rejoice with them that do rejoice, and weep with them that weep. Be of the same mind one toward another. Mind not high

things, but condescend to men of low estate. Be not wise in your own conceits. (Romans 12:9-16)

These passages speak for themselves, but I will repeat what I said earlier. When we grow in loving God and others, we will want to be able to give from God whatever He has available to help others. Many times we can give them from our natural abilities and talents. Often we need grace enablements that come only from God's Spirit. Love should always be our motive and it is the key to serving others. Love should therefore guide our discussion of the gifts.

The two lists of gifts

For to one is given by the Spirit the word of wisdom; to another the word of knowledge by the same Spirit; to another faith by the same Spirit; to another the gifts of healing by the same Spirit; to another the working of miracles; to another prophecy; to another discerning of spirits; to another divers kinds of tongues; to another the interpretation of tongues. But all these worketh that one and the selfsame Spirit, dividing to every man severally as he will. (1 Corinthians 12:8-11)

Having then gifts differing according to the grace that is given to us, whether prophecy, let us prophesy according to the proportion of faith; or ministry, let us wait on our ministering: or he that teacheth, on teaching; or he that exhorteth, on exhortation: he that giveth, let him do it with simplicity; he that ruleth, with diligence; he that showeth mercy, with cheerfulness. (Romans 12:6-8)

These are two different list of gifts that are given to the Body of Christ to enable us to serve one another. Some people call the list in Romans the motivational spiritual gifts to differentiate it from the list in 1 Corinthians. I don't have a problem with this classification, but I see something else. The list in 1 Corinthians is a list of gifts that are purely supernatural without the input of our soul. A person intent on understanding everything will probably place limitations on the Spirit of God in the expression of these gifts.

Individuals are made up of spirit, soul, and body. The Holy Spirit uses the human spirit and body and bypasses the mind in the gifts in 1 Corinthians 12. Paul speaks of this phenomenon concerning one of the gifts listed here, "For if I pray in an unknown tongue, my spirit prayeth, but my understanding is unfruitful" (1 Corinthians 14:14). We already discussed the possibility of the loss of control when we continue walking in things of the Spirit. It's the loss of control in which our minds cannot explain how, why, or even when these gifts are exercised. Some of us will refuse to go out into water that is over our heads. That's okay as long as others of us will brave the waters.

The list of gifts in Romans mentions teaching, which definitely signifies the use of the mind. It also lists cheerfulness and simplicity. These are other functions of the soul. Because one group of gifts uses the mind and other parts of the soul and the other group bypasses the mind does not mean one is superior or inferior to the other. It just means they are different.

Differences only give us a greater opportunity to perfect agape love in our lives. Like iron sharpening iron, differences between genders, cultures, and doctrinal beliefs all offer us an invitation to love with a love that is not natural. In the process, we are changed into the image of Christ. Ironically, that's what many of us want, but we often ignore the very invitation to be changed. We like the change that comes from a zap, not a journey that involves unconditional love.

Because members of the body believe differently about the exercise of these gifts does not mean one group is right and the other is wrong. We are members of one another. We need all the gifts of God available to us to move on up. Whether we individually exercise these gifts or not, we all benefit. Could it be God would have some of us go out into some of the deep things of the Spirit for the sake of the whole, but also will keep some of us with our feet on the ground, also for the sake of the whole? If that is a possibility, is it also possible that the whole Body would be stronger if we learned to fellowship together in spite of our different convictions. That would be a demonstration of love!

Four steps of ministry

We have seen the levels of walking in the Spirit. God wants to use us to serve, but there is a progressive development of service, or ministry. We will look at the Scriptures to see the four steps in the development of service.

The first step to serving God is awareness of our identity in Him. Next, we experience God's presence with us as He leads us. The third step in the development of service is a period of testing or trials. This period purifies our motives for service. It is a tough time, because it is very natural to serve God with selfish motives. Sometimes we stay in this wilderness of testing much longer than necessary because of the difficulty of learning to serve without pride or the need to be seen and recognized for what we do.

After we have finished this period of testing, we will come out prepared to minister in the full power of God's Spirit. We were able to use the gifts, powers, and abilities of God at the other levels, but our service after the testing is very different. The chart below shows these steps in the lives of Jesus, Paul, and the Christian believer.

	JESUS	PAUL	BELIEVER
1. Identity	Luke 3:21-22 Pleasing to the Father	Acts 9: 15-22 Vessel chosen to prove Christ	1 Cor. 1:30 Wise, sanctified, righteous and redeemed in Christ
2. Leading	Luke 4:1 Led by the Spirit	Galatians 1:17 Consulted the Spirit	Romans 8:35-39 Permanently connected to the Spirit
3. Testing	Luke 4:1-13 Tempted with success	2 Cor. 4:7-9 Tested with suffering	1 Peter 1:6-9 Tried by fire
4. Ministry	Luke 4:14-21 Empowered by the Spirit for God-given opportunity	1 Cor. 2:1-5 Weak flesh points to strong God	2 Cor. 3:6, 4:10-12 Manifesting the life of Christ; dying to self; Godly success through Spirit's intercession

Prayer:

Dear God, going out into the deep water has frightened me. I have not wanted to go off the deep end and I have not wanted to lose control. Help me to trust You to develop within me the powers and abilities You want to use to help others through me. Help me to let go of the control of my life, and turn it over to You.

CHAPTER 11

Levels of Spiritual Maturity

"As newborn babes, desire the sincere milk of the Word
that ye may grow thereby."

1 Peter 3:1

IN THE LAST CHAPTER, WE LOOKED at four levels of our
walk in the Spirit. This chapter introduces us to the work of
God's Spirit within us. The Holy Spirit is essential to the development of character and godliness within the believer. Many of the
works of the Holy Spirit have to do with His development within
us.

How do we begin this spiritual journey? We start by experiencing a new birth. We are born again of the Spirit by asking Jesus,
the Son of God, to come into our lives and take over. We accept
His death on the cross as payment for our sin and as the means of
reconciliation with God. Jesus Himself declared He was the only
way to God, the Father.

Jesus came to earth as an example of what God originally
intended. He was born of a virgin (Luke 1:27). He was the Word.
(John 1:1). He was born of the will of God (John 1:13). He was the
first to be born of incorruptible seed (1 Peter 1:4, 23). Of course,
there are differences between Adam (pre-fall) and Jesus. Adam was
made with a human spirit. The Holy Spirit overshadowed him, but
did not reside within him. Jesus is fully God. The life of God not
only surrounds Him, but is in Him and through Him. The first
Adam was made a living soul; the second Adam (Jesus) was made
a quickening (life-giving) spirit (1 Corinthians 15:45).

Through the death, burial, and resurrection of Jesus, the Tree
of Life is now made available to anyone who will receive it. Adam
could have eaten from the Tree of Life, but instead he ate of the

Tree of the Knowledge of Good and Evil. We, who came into this world with the knowledge of good and evil, can now partake of the Tree of Life through Jesus, who is life. We can now live out God's original purposes.

The identifying mark

Over the years, I have found that most people do not have a problem with the Jesus of Scripture. Most problems arise from those who claim to be His followers. How can we tell if someone really is a child of God? Something should indicate that a person is an authentic follower of God. The Scriptures say that others will know we are Christians by our love. The kind of love the Scriptures talk about is possible only to the extent one is controlled by God's Spirit. The amount of control the Holy Spirit has in the life of a Christian becomes the mark of the child of God. Unfortunately, many who claim to be Christians are not controlled by God's Spirit. Authentic Christianity is not man's search for God; it is God's search for man. Unfortunately, false Christianity is what turns a lot of people off from seeking the true God.

The difference between one who is a child of God and one who is not depends on the individual's decision to accept the gift of salvation which God makes available through Jesus, and that person's asking God to take over his or her life. This decision marks the beginning of an ongoing, vibrant relationship with God. This relationship with God—who is Spirit—involves communion based on a knowledge of God, intimacy with God, and trust in God. The relationship aspect is critical. It is not based on an idea about God, or a set of beliefs about God, or even an experience of God. Instead, it is man's spirit indwelled by God's Holy Spirit.

Before asking God to take over, everything in the individual's life is determined by how she feels, or what she thinks or desires—that is, by the realm of the soul. When a person asks God to take over, she essentially says, "I give up my rights to treat others selfishly or act the way I feel like acting. I will learn to act out of power and love in my spirit, empowered by God's Spirit. I subject my thoughts, feelings, and desires to the Word and will of God. I desire to learn how to live based on the help and direction of God."

We are spiritual babes because we give God limited control over our behavior. We do this because we have been used to controlling things based on our minds, wills, and emotions. Before the new birth, the human spirit lay dormant. Because our human spirit was non-functioning toward God, the soul has always acted more like an adult in the human personality as far as behavior and control are concerned.

The spirit, now indwelled by God's Spirit, is in the beginning stages of control over the individual. The Holy Spirit is not a baby. After the new birth, the human spirit empowered by the Holy Spirit begins to gain control over the human personality. Spiritual growth and maturity is the development of the Holy Spirit's control in the life of a believer. The progression to God's full control is depicted below.

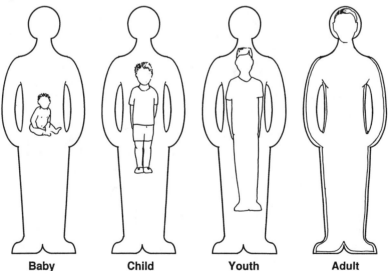

Baby   **Child**   **Youth**   **Adult**

I note four levels of spiritual development in believers. Other people may see more. Each of these levels is similar to human physical, social, intellectual, and emotional development, from infancy to adulthood.

Just as we saw a natural progression in our walk in the Spirit, there also is a natural progression of our development in spiritual character. There is a difference at each level. I do not believe we necessarily get more of the Spirit at different levels. In a way, the Spirit gets more of us. We were given everything from the Holy Spirit that we need at the time of our new birth. We are like a baby who is born with all the brain cells, muscles, organs, etc. that she will need, but she still is not capable of taking care of herself. That will come as she grows and progresses through each level of development.

Growing up is difficult. Churchianity is the ideal system for baby Christians that don't want to grow up. Professionals run the spiritual nursery, handing out bottles and pacifiers. Few are ever equipped to do the works of Jesus.

It is important to progress from infancy to adulthood. A Christian who stays a baby longer than normal is called a carnal Christian. The carnal or fleshly Christian is the second biggest detriment to authentic Christianity. Carnal Christians are the ones who loves to sing, "I don't want to grow up!" They refuse to do the Word. They prefer to keep their bottles. They want someone to constantly feed them. They are more comfortable hiring professionals to grow on their behalf. They are always learning, but never coming to the knowledge of the truth (2 Timothy 3:7).

Whatever level you are in your Christian walk: infant, child, youth, or adult, you can live in the Spirit. The more you live in the Spirit, the quicker you will mature to the next growth level. The main difference between young and mature Christians is consistency; the mature Christian operates consistently in the Spirit. The immature go there to visit, but are readily brought back to the flesh by some set-up or trap of Satan.

Setting us up to move back down

The enemy's first goal is to keep Christians from realizing they can live in the Spirit. He keeps them on a yo-yo, back and forth. But once a person finds out how to live in the Spirit, the enemy changes His plan. Now he has to set you up to upset you. Once you're upset, you'll try to lean on your own understanding, to figure out what or why this or that happened. Satan will play on your emotions of fear, anxiety, and insecurity. All of the above bring you out of the Spirit. You exit the place of rest, fail to trust in the goodness of God, and miss the peace that passes understanding.

Even mature Christians will get outside the realm of the Spirit. But they do not stay there long. They realize what happened, confess, and go back under God's control. The immature take much longer to figure out what happened. They may be out for weeks, months, even years. The tragedy is that few know they are out. Most still go to church and are deluded into believing their lives are pleasing to God.

Babyhood

Babyhood is not bad. We all start out there. The problem comes when we stop there. The first level of spiritual growth is infancy. When a Christian is born again, she is a new baby in Christ. Christ has entered her life, but the newborn Christian baby has not learned to give Christ full control of her actions. The Christian acknowledges the presence of Christ through the Holy Spirit. The newborn baby is responsible to grow by desiring and drinking the milk of the Word (1 Peter 2:2).

More mature believers in the Christian life are critical to the growth of baby Christians. The new believer needs the fellowship and relationships of other Christians in her life. She grows by watching more mature Christians model righteous behavior. This modeling takes place in the context of shared life experiences.

In Acts, new believers were right in the midst of believers who had actually been with Jesus. The older believers were up close and an integral part of the life of new believers. Meeting in homes, they ate together, prayed together, studied together, encouraged one another, and provoked one another to good works. This was all possible in the small-group setting of their assembling. The writer of Hebrews tells us not to forsake the kind of assembling that will allow us to provoke one another to good works. Are most of us able to do that at the Sunday morning service we call going to church? Could that be why no one is growing that much in "Church"?

A physical newborn baby cannot walk and must be carried everywhere she goes. Likewise, I believe the person who is a spiritual baby has to be carried by the Holy Spirit. A baby Christian does not know how to walk in the Spirit. She would literally be devoured by Satan if she were left on her own. She has to be cared for, fed, and cleaned up. The illustration below shows a picture of what the Holy Spirit's carrying of the newborn baby might look like:

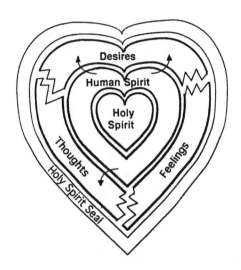

A spiritual babe wants what she wants when she wants it. She drinks the milk of the Word, unable to chew meat yet, and is unskillful concerning things of the Spirit. At this stage, Christians are immature and should not be given responsibility among the people of God. They have little spiritual discernment and are better guided by rules and regulations.

The task of the baby in Christ

- Desire the milk of the Word, drink it up, and grow.
- Fellowship with older believers in covenant relationships; that is, relationships in which you are accountable to others.

Childhood

As the influence of Christ grows in the life of a believer, she is considered a child in the Spirit. The influence of the Spirit in the life of a Christian who has progressed beyond infancy to the childhood stage is similar to the influence a child has over an adult. An adult will listen to a child's suggestion on what to do on the family vacation, but will not let the child control everything. The believer will listen to the Spirit of God, but will not give the Spirit full control. At this level, a lot of spiritual learning is taking place. She spends a lot of time in school. But because the Spirit is not in full control, the child continues to do what she wants to do based on the desires of her soul.

At this level, the Christian is immature in her spiritual thinking and speaking. She can be deceived very easily. She needs the assurance of her sins being forgiven. She needs discipline. She is considered a legal heir and joint-heir with Christ. All the promises of God belong to her by fact of the inheritance left by Christ, but she cannot benefit fully until she comes of age. Until then, she needs tutors (teachers) to supervise her.

The tasks of the child:

- Learn not to sin.
- Learn to abide in Christ.
- Stay away from idols.
- Learn to be not deceived.
- Learn to love in deed and in truth.

Youth

In the spiritual youth, the influence of the Spirit has grown. In fact, the youth can appear mature at times, because there is now a spiritual strength there that was not present in her childhood. She may exercise spiritual talents, such as discernment, but upon close examination, she still shows some immaturity. This is the stage where one must learn how to overcome the wicked one. Just as Jesus faced His greatest temptation in the wilderness, the spiritual youth also undergoes a time of testing. The youth has a spirit of independence, yet still needs supervision. Although she is beginning to show signs of maturity, she still needs adult input. Though she may be somewhat responsible, she is not yet ready to fully provide for herself.

Tasks of the youth:

- Learn submission.

- Become sober, responsible, and self-controlled.

- Learn to mortify deeds of the flesh.

- Learn to overcome the evil one.

Adult

The spiritual adult walks in the power of God and has mature understanding. She now has the ability to teach others. She is able to hear and understand the significance of God's Word and expound on it.

Spiritual adults know who they are. They have an intimate knowledge of the Father. They have grown up in all things. They offend not in word. They are patient. They love one another. Their senses have been developed to discern good and evil (Hebrews 5:14).

Spiritual adults can be held responsible for the growth of others. They know how to preach, warn, exhort, teach, comfort, and charge the children. They are not under ordinances. They have a Father Spirit in their hearts. Spiritual adults acknowledge oneness in the Body of Christ and have a desire for the whole body to grow up into unity in Christ. They are not under condemnation.

Their lives are led by the Spirit. They are matured sons of God.
They no longer walk after the flesh.

> There is therefore now no condemnation to them which are in
> Christ Jesus, who walk not after the flesh, but after the Spirit.
> For the law of the Spirit of life in Christ Jesus hath made me free
> from the law of sin and death. For what the law could not do,
> in that it was weak through the flesh, God sending his own Son
> in the likeness of sinful flesh, and for sin, condemned sin in the
> flesh: That the righteousness of the law might be fulfilled in us,
> who walk not after the flesh, but after the Spirit. For they that
> are after the flesh do mind the things of the flesh; but they that
> are after the Spirit the things of the Spirit. For to be carnally
> minded is death; but to be spiritually minded is life and peace.
> Because the carnal mind is enmity against God: for it is not
> subject to the law of God, neither indeed can be. So then they
> that are in the flesh cannot please God. But ye are not in the
> flesh, but in the Spirit, if so be that the Spirit of God dwell in
> you. Now if any man have not the Spirit of Christ, he is none of
> his. And if Christ be in you, the body is dead because of sin; but
> the Spirit is life because of righteousness. But if the Spirit of him
> that raised up Jesus from the dead dwell in you, he that raised
> up Christ from the dead shall also quicken your mortal bodies,
> by his Spirit that dwelleth in you. Therefore, brethren, we are
> debtors not to the flesh, to live after the flesh. For if ye live after
> the flesh, ye shall die: but if ye through the Spirit do mortify the
> deeds of the body, ye shall live. For as many as are led by the
> Spirit of God, they are the sons of God. (Romans 8:1-14)

Spiritual adults are needed in order for the whole Body to grow
up. A mature adult will use the privilege of prayer to help the
babies, children, and youth grow. That's why the prayer life of those
in leadership ministry is so critical. Paul prayed much for those in

different stages of spiritual growth. He has recorded some of the prayers he was led by God to pray.

Instruction in the Word, participation in caring for one another, up-close modeling of a consistently mature lifestyle, and prayer were the four components needed for spiritual maturity. No mattter where we may be, I thank God that He is able to grow us up in Himself. Let's seek Him with all of our heart.

When God has brought us to the place where He has all of our heart, the Holy Spirit seals the breaks. The Holy Spirit has worked His way through our souls to the place of covering our lives. This is a picture of the mature Christian's heart:

The proper environment for maturity

As more people in the Body of Christ mature to adulthood, we can recover and possibly go beyond where spiritual growth in the church stalled around 300 A.D. when Christianity became a state religion, priests were installed, and structures dedicated to this *new* religion were built. We will take a closer look at this in Chapter Eighteen.

It will take many spiritual adults to take back from Satan what he stole from Christians. As we move on up to Spirit living, we can grow from babyhood, to childhood, to youth, on to adulthood if we refuse to get trapped in religion. We've all fallen in the trap at some point or another. That's almost inevitable. Thanks to God's grace and mercy, we can be freed to continue on our journey. It will not be easy. In fact, the further we go, the harder it gets. I have a teen son who laments having to grow up, make decisions, and be responsible. I won't promise you or him a journey of ease, but I will tell you, you won't be bored. I've not arrived, but I'm on my way. We'll both learn together and be able to help bring others through infrequently charted waters.

Tasks for the adult:

- Continue to develop in the Word.
- Use prayer to help others grow.
- Restore others.
- Practice humility.
- Do the will of the Father.

Prayer:
Father, I don't know where I am in growth, but I'm probably not as far along as I thought I was. No matter where I might be right now, I want to move on up in maturity that I might be better able to help others. Please take me from where I am to the next level and keep on taking me all the way until I, like Paul, can say, "I have finished the course; I have kept the faith."

CHAPTER 12

Getting Spiritual

"I brethren, could not speak unto you as unto spiritual,
but as unto carnal, even as unto babes in Christ."

1 Corinthians 3:1

LIFE IN THE SPIRIT WILL NOT be life as usual. It will involve change, difficult change. If we are honest, most of us do not like change. But if we want change in our families, churches, communities, and cities, it has to begin with us.

Where Satan has used our plight to make us bitter, God wants to use it to make us better. We cannot change the pain of the past. We cannot change our ancestors' responses to injustice. We cannot change what others may think of us today. But we *can* change our walk, refusing to operate by the dictates of our thinking, emotions, and desires.

We can change our complaints to prayers. We can change our image of ourselves. We can see ourselves as God sees us—as spiritual beings. It is not so much who we are in Christ—though that is important—as who Christ is in us. When we place the emphasis on who we are in Christ, we emphasize ourselves. But when we place the emphasis on Christ in us, the focus is on Christ, where it belongs. His identity in us is what is important, not our identity. He is our hope of glory (Colossians 1:27). Christ is the sum of all spiritual things. Our victory is sealed; Christ is seated at the Father's right hand in the heavenly places (Ephesians 1:20). He is also preparing a place for us (John 14:2). In Christ is hid all the treasure of wisdom and knowledge (Colossians 2:3).

As you progress in the things of the Spirit, you can be a partaker of all Christ is. Will you let a change come over you? You are more than a conqueror. You have been bought by the precious blood of

Jesus. You are destined to overcome all the plans of the enemy. God has plans to use you; He is able to do great things in you and through you. You are loved! You are accepted in the beloved. You are God's child. You have been given everything that pertains to life and godliness (2 Peter 1:3). You have access to all of God's wisdom (James 1:5).

Changing of the trees

Our roots can change. We can be rooted and grounded in love; rooted and built up in Him, who is love. As we learn to walk in the Spirit, living a life of *agape* love for others and trusting in God, our hearts will stay together by the glue of the Holy Spirit. We will be uprooted from the Tree of the Knowledge of Good and Evil and replanted into the Tree of Life. The Holy Spirit of God brings wholeness to our hearts. When our hearts are integrated (whole), our desires, thoughts, and feelings work together.

Roots of Love
(Christ)

As we learn to walk in the Spirit, our tongues will come under the Spirit's control. Our tongues can then become a tree of life instead of a tree of death. "Rooted and built up in Him, and established in the faith, as ye have been taught . . . ." (Colossians 2:7)

Because we already are new creatures in Christ, we no longer have to walk in our old ways. We now have the power to walk in newness of life. Our physical roots may be anger, abuse, injustice, and slavery, but our spiritual root is the cross of Christ. We are no longer slaves to sin.

Because of Calvary, we have the ability to choose love. Because we have been born again of the Spirit, we have a new history–His story. The heavenly Father is now our ancestor. The new roots of love and our new ancestry take precedence over all of the ancestors in our natural family tree.

Change in our community

As Christ grows in us and as we grow in Christ, our identities and destinies will be in accord with His Word. We will not just have a head knowledge, but we will grow up into the Godhead. That will be the change that will make a difference in the world. Just as He lives to make intercession for us, our lives can be lived in intercession for those who so desperately need His grace and mercy.

If we live in the Spirit, we'll be able to say to the enemy, **"Enough, and no more!"** When we decide that the buck stops here, we can be instruments of change in our communities.

It is in an intimate relationship with the Spirit that we become effective women of God. That's where we become like Elijah, whose prayers availed much. That's where we have an open heaven–a hearing with God, but also hearing from God the enemy's plans for our homes, churches, and communities. That's how we stop the Devil and his evil work in our cities.

An overview of the process of getting there

We have talked about four levels of walking in the Spirit of God, and four levels of spiritual maturity. Both of these are important in order for us to be people of the Spirit. Now let us look at the process of moving toward living fully in the Spirit and being full of the Spirit.

To become people of the Spirit, we have to undergo several different growth operations. One is a division of the human spirit and soul by the Word of God. Another is a re-anchoring of our souls into the Spirit of God. This prepares us for the final process of moving the human spirit under the control of the Holy Spirit. It is through these processes of spiritual growth that we learn to walk by the human spirit empowered by the Holy Spirit, rather than by the old brokenhearted patterns of our flesh.

If we are properly connected to God through rebirth and are growing in our spiritual awareness, we should begin to express the habits of the Holy Spirit, which are love, joy, peace, contentment, and faith. We will do the things the Spirit of God does. We will pray for those who despitefully use us. We will bless those who curse us. We will sing and make melody in our hearts to the Lord, giving thanks to Him in all things. We will give to the poor, our families, and those in ministry. We will pray for the sick. We will fellowship with other believers. We will allow ourselves to be expressions of God's grace to others—works of faith, miracles, words of encouragement, or whatever is needed. Jesus said the works He did we would do if we believed in Him. He even said we would do greater works than those (John 14:12).

The human soul, with all its attachments, is what blocks the expression of the Spirit of God in our lives. It will be helpful to take a look at our soul before we continue to discuss spirituality.

The soul

The soul was designed to receive direction from our spirit. The soul is to be a servant, responding to the bidding and dictates of the S(s)pirit. The soul is the middle part of our being. It was designed to express what is in the spirit. It is here where the mind (intellect, memory, reasoning, thoughts, sensibilities) is renewed by the Word of God. The soul is used to being in control, but it is not meant to be in control.

When our spirit is cut off (separated) from God's Spirit, we do not enjoy the benefits of our spirit/soul connection. The soul has to lead and direct itself, without the Spirit's guidance. This is the principal root of all sin—independence from God. When the soul is in control, it seeks to maintain security through attachments other than to God. Without God as its anchor, our soul often enters into habits of sin, such as self-pity, self-will, self-preservation, pride, jealousy, covetousness, and complaining. The soul has a lot of anchors in which to (falsely) trust.

God orchestrates the removal of all of our props, securities, defense mechanisms, and idols until we have nothing left in the natural realm in which to trust. All we have left is in the spiritual realm, that is, Jesus and all of His fullness—His judgment, power, peace, strength, love, kindness, patience, and glory (Hebrews 12:25-29).

This process of shifting control can also be described as dying to ourselves. It involves much pain as we let go of all that we have depended upon and begin to trust only in Jesus to be our security, our worth, our acceptance, our comfort, and all that we seek. It is so painful that the soul would do anything to escape this death. Often, the soul will try to be religious in the strength of the mind, will, and emotions rather than let the Spirit have complete control. The majority of "Churchianity" is based on the religious strength of the soul instead of the leadership of the Spirit.

The Spirit

The spirit of man came from God, and it is responsive to God's Spirit. The Spirit of God is love within us and His power surrounding us. Man's spirit needs to be reconnected with the love of God in order to function properly. The spirit's purpose is to lead us. It receives its direction from God. It is the innermost part of man. It is God-conscious. It is the seat of our conscience, intuition, and communion. Its function is to have fellowship and communion with God, and to worship and seek to understand God. It is here that God regenerates, teaches, and leads us into His rest.

The Word of God is the means by which we become people of the Spirit. One cannot separate the Word of God from the work of God's Spirit. The Word divides between our soul and spirit, grows us up, washes us, and defines our spiritual walk (Hebrews 4:12; 1 Peter 2:2; Ephesians 5:26).

The spirit of man is initially enmeshed with man's soul. In order for the human spirit to be fully connected with the Holy Spirit and then be in a position under the guidance of the Holy Spirit to provide leadership to the soul, there has to be a separating of the spirit from the human soul. This separation is done by the Word of God (Hebrews 4:12).

The process that divides our soul and our spirit, allowing the Holy Spirit to take increasing control over our actions, begins with a series of trying circumstances that allow us to discern whether our actions are led by love or by selfishness—a focus on the soul. We have to go through situations in which the soul, void of the life of the Spirit, is unable to cope. When this happens, the Word of God divides between our soul and spirit and reveals to us areas in our lives that are still controlled by our soul. Perhaps our patience or faith will be tested. Rest assured that you will be tested in your area of weakness, so that you will learn to rely on the Spirit to advance spiritually. Each time we choose to go the way of the Spirit, we give the Spirit more dominance.

For this to happen, we must let the Spirit of God bring out what's in us. When we stop trying with our "soul strength" to do what God has told us to do, the Holy Spirit then can take over (2 Corinthians 12:9). This process happens over and over again in many areas of our life, until the "soul focus" is replaced by a dependency on the Spirit. Then, after all the props/anchors of the soul have been removed, and the human spirit and the soul have been separated, the next part of the growth process, in which we are re-anchored into God, can take place.

The re-anchoring of the soul

Once the soul has been separated from its anchors, it is now ready to be re-anchored into the human spirit, this time by the Holy Spirit of God. Now we are properly aligned to be led by the Spirit. We no longer make decisions based on feelings, thoughts, and desires, but our souls are subject to the desires, thoughts, and feelings of God's Spirit. Once the soul determines the will of the Lord, the soul and the body can carry it out. The difference spiritual growth makes is that the soul and body no longer dictate what we do and how we behave. Though behavior is determined by the soul, if the soul is properly connected to the Spirit of God, that Spirit becomes the source of one's behavior.

These are the things God is trying to work in our lives as He grows us up. Knowing what is going on will help us cooperate with Him in the process. That is the theory. Now let's talk about some of the things that take place in our lives as God is growing us up.

Prayer:

Father in Heaven, I desire to live in the Spirit. You alone know whether I am carnal or learning to grow in Your Spirit, but I suspect I have a ways to go. I can't get there by myself. I need Your help. You know the way. Take me there. When I accepted the gift of Your Son on (date)_____, I gave You the right to do everything You need to do to make me a vessel that You can use. Thank You that You will complete that which You have started in me.

CHAPTER 13

The School of the Spirit

" But is under tutors and governors until the time
appointed of the Father."

Galatians 4:2

GOD WANTS TO TAKE US TO A place in Him that is
under His shadow. It's the secret place of the Most High. It's
a place of Spirit living, a place of maturity in God's Spirit. Most of
us want to go to that place, but do not realize that getting there
takes going through another place that is rife with troubles and
trials. We start out to that secret place in the Spirit, but often will
turn around and come back when the going gets tough. No one
told us what it would take to get there. They only told us about all
the good things in that place. If you understand the process of
getting there, you'll understand a lot of what you're going through
in life.

When we spoke of the stages of walking in the Spirit and the
levels of spiritual maturity, the second to last stage or level both
suggested times of difficulty or testing. This dark night comes
before the dawn of God's glory. It's the wilderness we all have to
pass through after we leave Egypt (become saved) before we enter
the Promised Land (life in the Spirit).

In the school of the Spirit, we learn how to be the people that
God uses in this world. None of us naturally know the walk of the
Spirit. We have to learn how to lean on Jesus. We have to learn
how to walk in the Spirit and not fulfill the lust of the flesh
(Galatians 5:16). In the school of the Spirit we learn the ways of
God. It is important to learn what God desires to teach us as we
go through difficulties.

The fires and waters are the very difficult life experiences that we go through to get to that final place in the Spirit. Fire is an experience that consumes us; water is an experience that over-whelms us. These elements challenge us to our core, even to the point of our very trust in God. Sometimes they make us angry with God, or leave us wanting to give up on life. These experiences sap us of our natural ability to cope.

A method to this madness?

These experiences have purpose. They are designed to force us to a state of dependence upon the Spirit. They are strategically placed in our life to facilitate the division of the soul and human spirit. They are given to us to expose the anchors of our soul. It is in these times that we are given the opportunity to reaffirm the initial decision we made to surrender our lives unconditionally to Him. If we hesitate or refuse to do so, we get stuck. But God performs a work of radical "heart surgery." He remembers our first commit-ment, and uses the trials to work into us faith, wisdom, and a meek and quiet spirit—those qualities most precious to Him, and most rewarded by Him.

In the midst of our trials, God accomplishes many things in our lives, which we do not understand at the time. In fact, God appears schizophrenic to us: He tells us one thing and seems to do the opposite. The purpose of those trying times is to remove our desire to control our own lives. We may get a lot of trash thrown on us, but God recycles trash.

It is in the fires and the waters that we grow in grace and wisdom. It is where we learn to love, serve, obey, seek, and know God with our whole being. It is in the fires and the waters that we find what is in our house—is it thieves, or the fruit of the the Spirit? We must go through, not under or around, the experience. And, mercifully, the trial is temporary. God will deliver us. The result is a pearl of great price, worth selling our very lives to obtain. In the fires and waters, we are given the opportunity to really get to know God in a relationship with Him, not just to know about Him. Our knowledge goes beyond what we have heard; for our eyes now see Him (Job 42:5).

PRINCIPLES		KEY VERSE
When we are	We get to know God as	
Sick	Healer	James 5:14-16
Broke	Provider	Philippians 4:19
Anxious	Peace	Philippians 4:6-7
Weak	Strength	2 Cor 12:7-10
In a Battle	Defense	2 Cor. 20:1-12
Wicked	Righteous	1 Cor. 1:30

What happens in Trials:

- The ropes of bondage are burned off (Daniel 3:9–28)
- The self dies; the spirit is released (John 12:24)
- We have a ministry of comfort to others (2 Corinthians 1:3–10)
- Idolatry is exposed, and we are purified (Malachi 3:1–3)
- We are less prone to rely on the flesh (Romans 7:18)
- We have an intimate knowledge of God (Philippians 3:1–14)
- God becomes our defense (Zechariah 2:5)
- Our affections focus on things above (Colossians 3:1–3)

- Our hearts are perfected, established, strengthened, and settled (1 Peter 5:10)

Making sense of my wilderness years

I mentioned in an earlier chapter that God took me through a very trying time in my life. It was actually the beginning of several years of trials and tribulations. It was very uncomfortable; I did not like it all. But those years thrust me into the realm of God's Spirit, into a love that went beyond my natural inclinations and abilities. I had desired to walk in the Spirit, and thought knowing Scriptural principles such as "love covers a multitude of sins" was enough. But I had a rude awakening: knowing the Word was nothing in God's sight if we are not also doers of the Word!

The initial experience that brought judgment to my Christian maturity helped me to see that there was no good thing in me. I saw that even with my knowledge of the Word, spiritual gifts, determination, and service, I was carnal and not as mature as I thought I was.

As a result of a religious upbringing, I was well steeped in the knowledge of good and evil. Now I needed to live by the Tree of Life. In the midst of receiving the judgment of God, God made His love very clear to me. I was ready to receive it. I saw how all of my efforts to please God were not amounting to anything. I was ready to rely on what Christ had obtained for me on the cross.

Like the Galatians, I had been saved by the Spirit, but had tried to grow by the strength of my soul (Galatians 3:1-3). The years of trial were very painful and very humbling, but, looking back, I wouldn't trade those years for a billion dollars. I had to learn the futility of the Knowledge of Good and Evil so that I would lean upon the Tree of Life. I had no idea how anchored my heart was into things other than God. God used the many changes that took place in my life to bring my soul under the control of His Spirit.

There are two analogies of this process of developing the life of the Spirit. In this chapter we will consider the first one: going to school. The second analogy, boot camp, merits a chapter of its own.

The school of the Spirit

Students in school have to take tests to pass from one grade to the next. But I have some good news for you: you will pass your tests! You may not pass them the first time around. In fact, you may not pass them the second, third, or fourth time around. But if you are serious about God, He is serious about you. He will always give you a chance to take make-up exams. If you need one hundred tries before you pass the test, He will give them to you.

There are many tests. We will discuss only a few of these tests. One of the tests we must pass is the love test. All of us face love tests. Learning to walk in the Spirit is learning to love those whom we cannot naturally love with a supernatural love. God gives us chances to grow in love by putting people in our lives who are impossible to love in our own strength. These people test our love. When we find out we are unable to love them, we can go to the Father and draw upon His supernatural love. He is our strength in our weakness.

Who is your love test? Who in your life have you wished would change so you can respond to them in a more godly fashion? Maybe you have even prayed that God would change them. Have you asked God to change *you*? Maybe you are still trying to have that person removed from your life. It is important to know that many times irritating people have been put into our lives by God. Even if we change jobs, move, or leave, we'll probably get someone else placed in our life who is difficult to love until we learn to love with God's love. How do you respond to offensive people?

When someone offends you:

- Recognize your real enemy—Satan motivating the person to do wrong.

- Acknowledge that all things work together for good.

- Communicate with God through the Word, prayer, and fellowship to discern the purpose of what He has allowed.

- Communicate your feelings of anger, fear, etc. to God.

- Overcome evil with good. Do a kind act for the person or someone the person cares about.

- Commit yourself anew to God.

- Realize the offending person is really putting in a prayer request. (See explanation below.)

- Wait upon the Lord.

- Draw close to God in prayer and meditation on God's Word, especially 1 Corinthians 13.

Putting in a prayer request

Ever wonder why it seems everybody keeps bothering you? People who need prayer will often offend or persecute a person who is walking in the Spirit. According to the laws of the Spirit found in Matthew 5:44, those who offend us should get prayer from us. This is their way of putting in a prayer request. They are actually looking to offend a Spirit-living Christian, because, subconsciously, they know they'll get prayer as a result. The next time someone offends or persecutes you, just remember: they are putting in a prayer request.

Included in the love test is our love for and trust in God. Things will happen that will not make sense to us. It appears God does not love us. Our trust in the sovereignty of God will be severely tested. This is probably the most difficult test. Many turn back because of things that happen in their lives or the lives or those they love that are hard to reconcile with a loving God who is sovereign. These are times when it becomes so difficult we have to cry out to God to help us continue. There are times when we have to trust Him even when we don't understand.

God is trying to cultivate in us a trust in Him beyond our understanding. It is necessary that things we can't understand happen to us. God's purpose for us to live by the Tree of Life wouldn't be possible otherwise. Only God knows everything. There are some things He won't let us know. Our need to know why, what, when, how, or where about the things in our lives is an indication the soul still wants to be in control. The soul has a lot of problems surrendering control.

Who are you mad at?

The next test is the anger test. Whomever you consider your enemy will be the one against whom you will direct your anger. We pass this test when we understand that our real enemy is not the unloving person that gets to us; neither is God our enemy. Our real enemy is the hand that holds the "hammer." Understanding the real enemy behind the "hammer" and redirecting our anger at him is important. We mentioned this struggle in *Chosen Vessels*, but perhaps a visual illustration will help to make the point here.

Don't Attack the Tool

Is your tongue a deadly weapon?

The other test is the deadly weapons test. When our tongues are not under the full control of the Holy Spirit, our real enemy can manipulate circumstances in our lives to get us to use our tongues as deadly weapons.

Remember, we learned that the plan of the enemy is to steal the purpose God has given women by using the release valve of the tongue to deflate all God wants us to do. We saw earlier that the tongue functions like a release valve for the power and fruit of the Spirit in our lives. All the "air goes out of the balloon" when our tongues are used unwisely. When Satan has access to our tongues, he can stop the flow of the power of God. To be women of the Spirit it is critically important that our tongues get tamed.

What is happening in your life right now that is tempting you to murmur, complain, backbite, find fault, slander, or gossip?

That's your test. God wants you to pass this test by praying to Him, blessing others, encouraging others, and using your tongue to praise and thank God. According to 1 Corinthians 10, the people of God did not get out of the wilderness because they murmured and complained.

Though we should talk more to God than we do to others, it's okay to talk to others if you're sharing to receive godly counsel or encouragement. Talk to people who will keep you focused on the proper perspective. The Lord knows I don't need people who will make it easier for me to murmur, complain, or have a pity party. I can do all of that without much help. I think we all know the difference between sharing to receive pity, or to have a complaining buddy, and sharing because we sincerely desire to talk things out and find help in sorting out what our response to God should be.

Practical helps for going through

I find I do a lot of talking to myself when I'm going through a tough situation. That is usually unfruitful. It's unfruitful when we continue to go over all the "what if's" and "why's" again and again in our minds. We replay the situation more times than needed. We don't come away with peace. That's why we need to cultivate an attitude of praise and thanksgiving, no matter what happens. I have also found that music has been helpful to get and keep me in an attitude of praise. Jehosophat in 2 Chronicles 20 appointed singers. We can appoint Ron Kenoly or Morris Chapman or any other artist who will bring us into the spirit of praise and thanksgiving.

Music has also been used in my life to keep me pressing on. Once while traveling to speak, I had an accident on an icy road. That wouldn't have been so bad, but we had just got the car out of the shop because of an accident I had coming home from work after a midnight shift. (I really am not accident prone. In fact, those are the only two accidents I've had.) That was enough for me. I decided no more speaking for me. "I'm going home. Somebody else can do this." As soon as I got the car back on the road, the song that came on the tape we had playing was "I've come too far to turn back now." How was that for a coincidence? "Okay, Lord, I"I'll keep pressing on." (By the way, even though the car knocked over a mailbox, there was not one scratch on the car.)

It is important to think on things that are above (Colossians 3:2). The things we should think on are listed for us: things that are true, noble, just, pure, lovely, of good report, virtuous, and praiseworthy (Philippians 4:8).

Your boss may be unfair, but don't waste your time thinking about how unfair he or she is. That will give you a complaining spirit. Concentrate on the fact that you are employed. Find something good about your boss to think about. Maybe they are unfair in assignments, but generous in giving raises. Maybe he or she has a lot of compassion for people. Maybe he is a family man. If none of these fit, your assignment is to find something good about the person and think on those things when he or she comes to your mind. Those of you who think you've been let off the hook because you don't have a boss or a problem with one, substitute a mother-in-law, daughter, son, neighbor, husband, neighbor's dog, or whoever it is in your life that is causing irritation.

I have been led to do something nice to people who hurt me. This keeps me from getting bitter. It does not make a lot of sense, but it is a spiritual principle that works. It is even more helpful to do the act of kindness anonymously. Certainly, we should pray for people who persecute us and despitefully use us (Matthew 5:44).

It's important to keep pressing on no matter what happens. Remember, Satan does not want you to get to the Promised Land. He's been allowed to put these things in your life to get you to turn around and stop pursuing the things of the Spirit. He knows that when God is finished taking you through the fires and waters, you will come out as pure gold and will be able to do damage to his kingdom. Don't think he's going to let you waltz on through the wilderness to the Promised Land.

You need the help of your family

Solicit the help of others as you go through. There have been times I would not have made it if I had not called on someone else to pull me through. It was humbling to admit I could not do it on my own, but that's why God has placed us in a family. My friend Brenda helped me a lot when my family was in Nigeria.

I've found that a walk with God can only be lived out in its fullness in real open, transparent fellowship with others. This sort of fellowship has to be under the leadership of His Holy Spirit. For me, at times it has been at regular times of prayer and sharing, most other times it has been spontaneous sharing and praying. Sometimes it has taken place in person. Some of the time over the phone or even through the mail. But God has given wisdom and direction for it all. The word of God says where two or three are gathered together in His name, He is in the midst (Matthew 18:20).

> And let us consider how we may spur one another on toward love and good deeds. Let us not give up meeting together, as some are in the habit of doing, but let us encourage one another—an all the more as you see the Day approaching. (He brews 10:24,25)

A major part of our growth is allowing God's grace to work in us so that we are able to humbly face our faults, sins, weakness, and carnal tendencies. We need to be constantly aware of the futility of our lives apart from the life of Christ. But we must now go one step further. To be completely healed, we must be willing to share our faults with other member of the body so that they can cover us in prayer. "Confess your faults one to another, and pray one for another that ye may be healed" (James 5:16). We won't move on up to Spirit living if we don't risk being transparent with other members of our spiritual family.

It is God's intention that we learn to be joined to one another in forms of body life ministry such as prayer, encouragement, burden sharing, and as we have already mentioned, confessing our faults one to another. This is an essential part of our life together as a body. God has joined us to one another. We need each other much more than we recognize. "From whom the whole body fitly joined together and compacted by that which every joint supplieth" (Ephesians 4:16).

Just recently, as I was going through a difficult time, I called a friend of mine. She shared some things with me and challenged me to be bold. She already knows I struggle with passivity and fear. Many other times God has led me to share my struggles and request prayer from others.

Ready for graduation

All of the tests have one thing in common: they are impossible to pass with our own souls (mind, will, and emotions). They force us to learn the life of the Spirit, and to lean on Jesus. They force us to give up our own understanding and acknowledge Jesus for His help in our weakness (Proverbs 4:5,6). Jesus has already passed the tests. All He wants to do is bring you to the end of your own rope so that you will let Him take the test for you. Some of us have been taking the same test for years because we have not relied on God to take our tests for us. Will you admit to God now that you are in desperate need of His help to pass your tests?

We have finished school. It is time to go to work. And what is the work we have prepared to do? Our work is to fight the real enemy of our souls, on the battlegrounds we mentioned previously. The next chapter shows us how we develop as spiritual warriors.

Prayer:

Father, sometimes I don't see how You can do all that needs to be done in my life, but I am confident You are able to do exceedingly abundantly above all I can ask or think. Change me so I can be an instrument of change. Teach me how to lean on Jesus so He can pass my test for me. Breath of life, breathe on me.

CHAPTER 14

Spiritual Boot Camp

*"Yea, though I walk through the valley of the shadow of death,
I will fear no evil: for thou art with me; thy rod and thy staff
they comfort me."*

Psalm 23:4

WOMEN ARE CALLED TO BE SPIRITUAL warriors in the spiritual battle we all have to fight. We are called to be strong soldiers in the army of God, marching against the enemy of our souls.

Some women have to use their spiritual energy to fight conflict within the church. Others have to fight to keep or get their sons and daughters off drugs. Some have to fight a husband's infidelity. Many women are fighting diseases. These are legitimate battles. They often prepare us for spiritual warfare. As we go to the place of living in the Spirit, God allows us to fight the Amorites and Hittites as part of our boot camp experience preparing our hands for war (Psalm 144:1). But God's purposes for giving us these battles is to help us learn how to truly turn our battles over to Him.

We must learn to let God fight our battles. He is able! When we refuse to let Him fight for us, we lose. Frustrations abound when we fight our own battles.

Some women fight people in leadership positions. This is the wrong battle. We should always direct our fight against spiritual powers, never against people. We are to love people, praying God's mercy and grace upon them. With people we are to have a meek and quiet spirit (1 Peter 3:4).

The spiritual warring spirit of women can easily be misdirected, however. With all of the fighting we do, we could be losing the real battle. There's battles for our families, our children, our churches, and our relationships. There is a battle for truth and justice. God has called women to take a part in winning these battles, but most of us haven't even gotten around to fighting them yet.

Instead, we are battling for equal rights, worth, purpose or the right to control our own destinies. We're guilty of fighting battles Jesus already won for us. Jesus determined our worth by purchasing us with His precious blood. Jesus chose us as vessels of honor. He gave us purpose—a destiny that joins us with Him.

When we fight the wrong battles, those around us lose out, too. That's what Satan planned. The hope for our families, neighborhoods, cities, and this nation lies in women fighting the real enemy. As a neighbor, aunt, Sunday School teacher, or mother,

God would have us fight the real enemy that stands behind the school bully, neighborhood crack house, or perpetrator of violence. By not understanding what it is to live in the Spirit, we are not equipped to fight the real enemy.

Preparing for war

All soldiers have to go through boot camp before they can go to war. We did not get saved just to sit around and have a good time. In our Christian infancy, we do not have a lot of responsibility, but after we grow, there is much work for us to do.

We got saved to be partners with God in destroying the works of the enemy. If our purpose for getting saved was just to go to heaven, we all could have gone on home immediately after getting saved. Our work is to be soldiers in the army of God. To be trained, soldiers need to go to boot camp.

I asked Curtis Johnson, an army veteran to describe boot camp to me. He mentioned survival as the key. The drill sergeant, as the person in charge of the company, becomes everything to you: mother, dad, best friend. He's with you from start to finish. His job is to equip you for battle. The system is similar to slavery; you are bought and owned by Uncle Sam.

This army veteran listed the following purposes of boot camp:

- Get into shape.
- Learn to use weapons.
- Learn to take orders.
- Prepare for combat in hostile environments.
- Work as a team: Look out for fellow soldiers.

Those are the same purposes for spiritual boot camp. The person who has gone through spiritual boot camp and is ready to go to war is:

- In shape spiritually.

- Trained to use the Sword of the Spirit as well as other spiritual weapons.

- Quick and ready to obey all orders.

- Living and walking in the protection of the Spirit.

- Cognizant of her need for and responsibility toward others.

In boot camp, one goes through many trials and tribulations. Some experience infirmity and even different kinds of death. These experiences should not surprise us. We are told of them all through the Word of God.

Trials

Beloved, think it not strange concerning the fiery trial which is to try you, as though some strange thing happened unto you: But rejoice, inasmuch as ye are partakers of Christ's sufferings; that, when his glory shall be revealed, ye may be glad also with exceeding joy. If ye be reproached for the name of Christ, happy are ye; for the spirit of glory and of God resteth upon you: on their part he is evil spoken of, but on your part he is glorified. But let none of you suffer as a murderer, or as a thief, or as an evildoer, or as a busybody in other men's matters. Yet if any man suffer as a Christian, let him not be ashamed; but let him glorify God on this behalf. For the time is come that judgment must begin at the house of God: and if it first begin at us, what shall the end be of them that obey not the gospel of God? And if the righteous scarcely be saved, where shall the ungodly and the sinner appear? Wherefore let them that suffer according to the will of God commit the keeping of their souls to him in well doing, as unto a faithful Creator. (1 Peter 4:12-19)

Webster's Collegiate Dictionary, Tenth Edition defines trials as "a test of faith, patience, or stamina through subjection to suffering." *Vine's Dictionary* defines trial as "a refining."

I have a friend who is going through physical pain. It is difficult, and she has had to cling more firmly on to the Word of God for strength. She has had to rely on the prayers of fellow Christians. Through this trial of her faith, she has learned more of the faithfulness of God. She is more skilled in the use of the Word of God as a weapon to defeat fear when it assaults her mind. She has drawn closer in her relationship to God. She has learned to obey Him, even when it appears impossible. She is becoming a ready warrior in God's army. The Holy Spirit is becoming everything to her. He is equipping her to be able to rescue many others from Satan's clutches.

Tribulations

> And not only so, but we glory in tribulations also: knowing that tribulation worketh patience; and patience, experience; and experience, hope: And hope maketh not ashamed; because the love of God is shed abroad in our hearts by the Holy Ghost which is given unto us. (Romans 5:3-5)

Webster's Collegiate Dictionary, Tenth Edition defines tribulation this way: "to press, oppress; distress or suffering resulting from oppression or persecution." *Vine's Dictionary* defines it as "to be afflicted."

I have another friend who is being oppressed and persecuted because of her stand on the Word of God. Sometimes, it is so difficult that she wonders about God's love. But she realizes that she is being trained for war. She sees much of the pain that women are in, and as God uses her to minister to their pain, she knows the difficult experiences she is undergoing are helping her minister with sincerity and understanding.

As she is being pressed and oppressed, God is using her experience to press her more into Himself. Sometimes, in the squeeze, ungodly thoughts and attitudes come out. God is continuing to purify her. She, too, is learning to be quick and ready to obey all orders. She is becoming trained in using the spiritual weapon of fasting. She is getting into spiritual shape by having to spend more time seeking God's wisdom.

Infirmities

> And he said unto me, My grace is sufficient for thee: for my strength is made perfect in weakness. Most gladly therefore will I rather glory in my infirmities, that the power of Christ may rest upon me. Therefore I take pleasure in infirmities, in reproaches, in necessities, in persecutions, in distresses for Christ's sake: for when I am weak, then am I strong. (2 Corinthians 12:9-10)

Webster's Collegiate Dictionary defines infirmity as "the condition of being feeble; frailty." The *Vine's* definition says infirmity is most frequently "want of strength, weakness; inability to produce results."

A little while ago, as I was preparing to speak somewhere, I received some devastating news that left me very weak. I did not see how I would have the strength to minister to others. I knew that I was incapable of producing results in the frame of mind the news left me. I called some friends and asked them to activate a chain of prayer.

The Lord worked in a powerful way that weekend. I came away with a new sense of the awesome power of God. I knew it was not about me. I had been very weak. But I could also understand how Paul could say he delighted in weakness, because God's strength was made perfect. I'm angry enough at the enemy that if it takes weakness to bring defeat to him in the lives of people, so be it. I, too, learned more about my need for others. I really felt the strength of those who were praying for me.

Dying

> Always bearing about in the body the dying of the Lord Jesus, that the life also of Jesus might be made manifest in our body. For we which live are always delivered unto death for Jesus' sake, that the life also of Jesus might be made manifest in our mortal flesh. So then death worketh in us, but life in you (2 Corinthians 4:10-12).

Webster's— death is " to expire, pass out of existence; to subside gradually; to cease functioning." *Vine's*—"deadness."

Death is experienced in many ways. We die daily to our reputation, hopes, and dreams. We die to always knowing what is going on in our lives. We lose control over how our lives are going to go. I have friends who have experienced death to their career plans. Others have experienced death to relationships and even marriages. I personally experienced the death of two family members in 1995, within eleven months of each other.

I sorely miss my mother and my only sister. Those relationships have ceased to function. I won't deny 1995 was a difficult year. But God's grace has been sufficient. I have literally been sustained by the prayers of friends and partners. I owe my sanity to the grace of God.

It is comforting to know that while death may be working in our lives in many ways, life is being poured into the lives of others. Death is not as bad as it seems when you know resurrection follows.

Boot camp prepares us for war. When we make it through boot camp, we have learned to lean on Jesus. We live under His wings.

Clothed in His armor, we are strong soldiers in God's army. With our shield we are able to keep away the wiles of the enemy. We have been forced to use fasting as a means of moving from the flesh to the Spirit, so when God leads us to fast as a means to undo yokes, we're ready (Isaiah 58:6).

In boot camp, we go through many trials, tribulations, infirmities, and death. We are weak and tempted to give up. This process is necessary in order for God's Holy Spirit to gain control. We have no idea how much control we try to keep over our own lives. That's part of the flesh. It's not until we go through trials that God is able to take the strength out of our will. This process of boot camp is necessary because God wants to take our ways and will out of us and to put His ways and will into us.

> Then the LORD put forth his hand, and touched my mouth. And the LORD said unto me, Behold, I have put my words in thy mouth. See, I have this day set thee over the nations and over the kingdoms, to root out, and to pull down, and to destroy, and to throw down, to build, and to plant. (Jeremiah 1:9-10)

God wants to root out our old way of doing things.

> For my thoughts are not your thoughts, neither are your ways my ways, saith the LORD. For as the heavens are higher than the earth, so are my ways higher than your ways, and my thoughts than your thoughts. (Isaiah 55:8-9)

God has to pull down our tendency to lean on human understanding.

> Trust in the LORD with all thine heart; and lean not unto thine own understanding. In all thy ways acknowledge him, and he shall direct thy paths. (Proverbs 3:5,6)

The final thing that happens in boot camp is removing our attachments. We talked about god substitutes or attachments in the first part of this book. It is in the fires that the ties to our attachments are burned away.

God becomes everything to us as each of the idols or god substitutes in our lives are removed. We can truly say, "There is only one God and there is none like YOU." We will truly worship God out of a pure, whole heart.

"I am the LORD thy God, which have brought thee out of the land of Egypt, out of the house of bondage. Thou shalt have no other gods before me." (Exodus 20:2-3)

God does not stop with rooting out, pulling down, and destroying. He also builds and plants. In exchange for our ways, he plants His ways into our lives.

> This I say then, Walk in the Spirit, and ye shall not fulfill the lust of the flesh. For the flesh lusteth against the Spirit, and the Spirit against the flesh: and these are contrary the one to the other: so that ye cannot do the things that ye would. But if ye be led of the Spirit, ye are not under the law. (Galatians 5:16-18)

As God continues to work with us, He plants His thoughts into our thinking. We begin to lean on His understanding, instead of our own.

God then begins to build His strengths into us.

> Hast thou not known? Hast thou not heard, that the everlasting God, the LORD, the Creator of the ends of the earth, fainteth not, neither is weary? There is no searching of his understanding. He giveth power to the faint; and to them that have no might he increaseth strength. Even the youths shall faint and be weary, and the young men shall utterly fall: But they that wait upon the LORD shall renew their strength; they shall mount up with

wings as eagles; they shall run, and not be weary; and they shall walk, and not faint. (Isaiah 40:28-31)

We can cooperate with God's plan in the midst of boot camp. When we do, we can get through much quicker. When we understand we are the clay and He is the potter, we will cease murmuring and complaining when we do not understand why things are so hard. God is becoming dominant and self is losing in the war for control of our lives.

In order to allow the full work of God in our lives, it is essential that we surrender everything to Him. We are not our own. We have been bought with a price. It is only reasonable that we acknowledge the fact that He owns us and everything we possess. If we lose our reputation, friends, possessions, career plans, hopes, etc. in the fire, it should not matter because we had given all of those up to God anyway. We learn to say, "Oh, well."

We mentioned in the last chapter that we have to cultivate attitudes of thanksgiving and praise. We see in the passage below that giving thanks is part of our ability to be people of the Spirit.

In everything give thanks: for this is the will of God in Christ Jesus concerning you. Quench not the Spirit. Despise not prophesyings. Prove all things; hold fast that which is good. Abstain from all appearance of evil. And the very God of peace sanctify you wholly; and I pray God your whole spirit and soul and body be preserved blameless unto the coming of our Lord Jesus Christ. Faithful is he that calleth you, who also will do it. (1 Thessalonians 5:18-23)

When we go through to the place of the Spirit, we will come out strong in the Lord and in the power of His might. Ephesians 6:10 says, "Finally, my brethren, be strong in the Lord, and in the power of his might." We will also be able to say with the psalmist,

"Blessed be the LORD my strength, which teacheth my hands to war, and my fingers to fight" (Psalm 144:1).

Love is the weapon

Living in the Spirit is living in light and living in love. We get to learn how to use spiritual weapons in boot camp. God's *agape*, unconditional love stops the enemy dead in his tracks. It stops the enemy's plan to continue hurt and pain. The question is, do we obey God and the rules of the Spirit in our lives that are filled with pain and rejection? Do we bless when others curse us? We can choose to keep pain alive by using our tongues to hurt someone else; or we can choose to stop our pain by taking it to God, and taking the wrongs done to us by others to the cross.

We have a choice. We can take the high road or the low road. The choice boils down to walking in forgiveness or walking in bitterness. Do you walk in the Spirit or do you walk in the flesh? Walking in the Spirit requires spiritual understanding (1 Corinthians 2:14). Living in the Spirit means using spiritual weapons to fight against Satan's attacks. We cannot afford to use the same weapons Satan supplies us to fight against Satan.

For the weapons of our warfare are not carnal, but mighty through God to the pulling down of strongholds. Casting down imaginations and every high thing that exalts itself against the knowledge of God, and bringing into captivity every thought to the obedience of Christ. (2 Corinthians 10:4)

The weapons of love, forgiveness, prayer, and blessing others will indeed hit their intended targets. Just as Satan had the equation to bring defilement to our tongues, God has the arithmetic equation to bring our tongues back to the service of His original purpose. Walking in the Spirit will bring healing to our hearts. Walking in the Spirit will root and ground us in God's love. God's arithmetic equation will bring life out of our tongues.

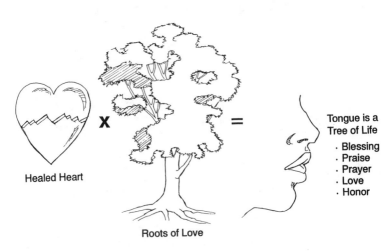

Healed Heart

Roots of Love

Tongue is a
Tree of Life

· Blessing
· Praise
· Prayer
· Love
· Honor

Weapons of love, forgiveness, and speaking well of others can only be formed in us through abandonment to and total dependence on God. Many Christians forgive and bless mechanically, and not with a whole heart. This is only the "arm of the flesh" in action.

A friend of mine who has been severely emotionally wounded by a Christian husband who divorced her, tells me that there have been times when she was so overwhelmed with the mandate to move on up that she decided that she **could not** and **would not** move on up if it required having to walk in love with her ex-husband. She felt she just couldn't do it and would rather give up and ask God to take her on home to heaven. But—even when she was at her lowest points—she was overwhelmed by God's mercy and patience. She has been made aware that her heavenly Father knows the depth of her pain. She is glad the Father does not give her pat answers like, "Just forgive him by faith." She has seen how she truly can do all things through Christ who strengthens her (Philippians 4:6). She has experienced God's presence and strength every seemingly impossible step of the way as she chooses to go up higher.

She has learned that a major hindrance to obeying God's command to love unconditionally is her own unwillingness to do so. She says, "It wasn't that I could not do what God told me to do in His strength, it's just that it went against every cell of my being. I just did not want to. But once I lined my will up with His, I found I could."

Perhaps an actual illustration of how God has worked in her life will help make the point. After her husband—who had admitted being unfaithful—decided to divorce her, they still lived together in the same apartment for a while. They didn't eat, talk, or do anything else together. One day, he came into the apartment, under the attack of a debilitating disease that paralyzed half of his body. Because of the hurt, rejection, and lack of help he had given her when she was ill, it would have been natural for her to think, " You're getting what you deserve. Who do you think is going to help you now." Instead, She found herself thinking about the fact that he needed to eat. She looked at him and out of her mouth popped the words, "Are you hungry? Can I get you something to eat?" She went into her bedroom and literally rolled her eyes up at God, and said, "You want me to do **what**?" Then she heard her mind repeat a lesson she had been trying to get across to her young son, "When I tell you to do something, I want you to do what I tell you to do!" Reluctantly, she whispered, "Yes, Lord." For the rest of that week in God's strength, she nursed him back to health.

This story does not have a "storybook" ending. This friend finally did suffer the pain of divorce, and even currently has "opportunities" to be pulled from the Spirit over child support and visitation issues. But she is learning that God is her only completely trustworthy source of supply. She finds she has to continuously lean on God for wisdom and many other things she once took for granted. Through it all, she is learning the incalculable value of unconditional love—God's love for her and His ability to love through her.

When you have learned the power of unconditional love and forgiveness, you may want to encourage others to forgive and love unconditionally. This same friend has the following suggestion, born out of her experience:

> It's important when we are led to encourage others to forgive and go on that we make sure we have spent time in God's presence. We should ask God to "tenderize" our hearts so that we won't come off sounding callous as we encourage another to forgive. Some people have had horrendous things done to them. Though it is important for their own sakes to forgive and let go of bitterness and resentments, they need to know that even if no one else understands how difficult it is, God does.

I think that is good advice. We need to speak the truth to each other, but let's do it in love, giving large doses of mercy.

When we endure, obeying God's Word when it is difficult, God mends our broken hearts. As we learn to walk in the Spirit,

God—by His Holy Spirit—holds the pieces of our hearts together. As we learn humility in and through the trials we go through, God comes near to us. You see, God loves a broken heart that is contrite. A broken heart that is proud will experience all the negative results we spoke of earlier. A broken heart that is humble is an asset to Spirit living. In humility, we know we have nowhere else to go but to God. God is nigh unto those with broken and contrite hearts (Psalm 51:17).

Prayer:

Father, I don't like the fires and the waters I am now in. But I do want You to complete in me the work that You started. I want to get to know You better. I want You to convict me if I begin to complain or murmur about my circumstances. I want You to remind me of my commitment to go through whatever it takes to be conformed to the image of Your dear Son, Jesus. I give You permission to draw me back if I turn away from You at any time.

SECTION IV

Life After The Spirit

CHAPTER 15

The Powers that Be

"Power belongeth unto God."

Psalm 62:11

THE SPIRIT-FILLED, SPIRIT-LED woman is connected to the power of God Almighty. Under God's supervision, she uses the power of God to bring change to the chaos in this world. It is important for women to understand power, because sometimes what we think is God's way of using power is really not.

There are four major forms of power that bring change into the lives of others: (1) the power of control, (2) the power of authority, (3) the power of influence, and, (4) the power of loving service. This is the order mankind has given to the importance of power. We will look at them in this order, but we will see that the order should actually be reversed. When we emphasize loving service first, and then the power of influence, we will be given the power of authority in the spiritual realm and can participate with God through the power of control.

God is the source of all power. All dominion, power, and authority belong to Him (Psalm 62:11; Psalm 147:5; Matthew 6:13). *Dominion* is defined as "supreme authority; sovereignty; absolute ownership." Within the power of supreme authority is the ability to create, to change people, to change circumstances, and to rule the unseen. It's the power that God alone holds.

Think about the power of God. God's power created the world, the galaxies, and all the universe. His power upholds the world right now. God's power brings conviction and change. God's power heals. His power is above all the power of the enemy.

God alone has the ultimate power of control, but He has given dominion to both men and women as partners with Him. In Genesis 1:26-27, God divided the powers:

> And God said, Let us make man in our image, after our likeness: and let them have dominion over the fish of the sea, and over the fowl of the air, and over the cattle, and over all the earth, and over every creeping thing that creepeth upon the earth. So God created man in his own image, in the image of God created he him; male and female created he them. And God blessed them, and God said unto them, Be fruitful, and multiply, and replenish the earth, and subdue it: and have dominion over the fish of the sea, and over the fowl of the air, and over every living thing that moveth upon the earth. (Genesis 1:26-28)

The power of authority

The second power, the power of authority, also is a power that God shares with humans. God originally gave mankind power to rule over His creation. After the fall, ruling power was also exercised over people. I do not believe that was God's original plan. I believe God originally gave ruling power to humans to be used over the animal creation and also over demonic powers.

In any event, ruling power is now used over people. The power of authority is ruling power: someone is in charge, making decisions and telling others what to do. Ruling power is the power the boss has at work. It's the power used by many husbands over their wives, parents over their children, and pastors use over their churches.

In *Fatal Conceit,* a book which depicts some of the things that went wrong at Heritage, USA, author Richard W. Dortch says, "Power denotes inherent ability of the admitted right to rule and govern others—to determine what others will and will not do."[1] Although this world looks at the power of authority as controlling others, in reality, only God has the power of control. I believe the authority God gave us over each other is really to be exercised as loving service along with the power of godly influence.

Ruling power has been perverted by the enemy of God. Both men and women exercise ruling power in its perverted state, but men tend to have more opportunities to do so. More men are bosses, in charge of organizations, divisions, offices, churches, etc. It is very important to exercise the duties that the world's system of ruling power gives with a loving servant attitude in order not to use power in ways that are ungodly.

People with power of authority or ruling power have some limited power of control, but they are accountable to God in the use of that power. There is a lot of potential to abuse ruling power and bring hurt and damage to those under one's authority.

Ruling power can bring outer change. Your boss can tell you to take only a half hour for lunch. You can tell your child that he can't drive the car. Your pastor can tell you that you have to follow the proper protocol in order to use the church facility. Many people will outwardly follow the orders or dictates of those in control because they want to keep their jobs, their marriages, and their relationships. Inside, they harbor resentments, rebellion, and bitterness. Ruling power can change actions, but not hearts.

Because ruling power is decision-making power, it is often used to hamper or keep women down. People in positions of ruling power often base their decisions on what benefits themselves or those whom they like. People in positions of authority have used their power to discriminate against African Americans and other minorities. African American women in particular have been oppressed and even abused by the perverted use of ruling power. It's no wonder that many women strive for that kind of power. We hope thereby to get vengeance, demand our due respect, and live above abuse and oppression.

A friend of mine who is in management told me of a situation on her job in which she was being undermined, largely because she was an African American woman. Men who were used to being over African Americans and women were having a hard time taking instructions from her. I'm sure other minority women can relate similar stories. Someone else I know told of giving a suggestion on her job and being ignored, but when someone else gave the exact same suggestion, all of a sudden he was a hero. Over the years, my husband has had incidents at work when those under him resist taking directions from him because he is black.

The structure of ruling power

Ruling power has a hierarchical structure. Someone is at the top while others are at the bottom. The ones underneath are at the mercy of those above them. The ones at the top see the ones under them as the means of obtaining *more* (power, money, prestige, position, recognition, etc.). That tempts them to use and abuse those underneath. It's a temptation inherent in a hierarchical system. Fortunately, not all people in positions of ruling power succumb to this temptation.

Most systems of organization in the civilized world are ruled by a hierarchical power structure. Whether you work in government, the military, education, social services, or corporate America, you will run into this system. It's an efficient way to get things done and many great things have been accomplished by this power system. Perhaps in this fallen world it is the only system that will work. But it was not God's original plan for humans, and certainly is not His plan for governing His own family. God's plan was for His family to ruled by servant leadership. Hierarchical power originates in the angelic chain-of-command system. Consider this quote from *Climb the Highest Mountain* by Gene Edwards:

Heaven had the following structure: God. Free. Without law. No restrictions. Above even liberty. As Creator He is by nature King. Lord. Ruler and Potentate. Beneath are the angels. He divided this angelic host into three equally numbered divisions. Over each of these three divisions He set a glorious archangel. Take a look at that. What do you see? God had set up the original *chain-of-command!*

One of those three archangels led a revolt in the Heavenlies. For this insurrection he was cast out of the heavens to the earth. With him went his legions . . . Lucifer came to the regions around earth. He led the fallen angels with him. They came according to inherent order. Behold, organization got to earth by *treason*. Organization was never intended for planet earth. It is an alien thing. It is foreign to earth and to man. . . . Man, like God in whose image he was created, was not designed to be systematized, organized, or controlled. Man, like God, was made for total freedom. Man was not ordained to be controlled or ruled. Man—like God—was to rule![2]

Gene Edwards insists Lucifer brought this system of organization into the human race to keep man from having his attention and dependence upon God. He defines the angelic system of organizations as what the Scripture refers to as "the world system."

Watchman Nee in his book *Love Not the World*, defines the world system as an ". . . orderly arrangement or organization . . ."

Behind all that is tangible we meet something intangible, we meet a planned system; and in this system there is a harmonious functioning, a perfect order. . . .There is, then, an ordered system, 'the world', which is governed from behind the scene by a ruler, Satan.[3]

The Scriptures tell us: "The whole world lieth in the evil one" (1 John 5:9). To participate in the world order is to put ourselves in the lap of the evil one. Watchman Nee says,

> Satan well knows that, generally speaking, to try to ensnare real Christians through things that are positively sinful is vain and futile. They will usually sense the danger and elude him. So he has contrived instead an enticing network, the mesh of which is so skillfully woven as to entrap the most innocent of men. [4]

The sad point about this whole pattern is that everything that operates under this structure actually operates under Satan himself. He is in ultimate control of everything that is patterned after what the Bible calls the world system.

The tragedy is that the church has bought into the world system of organization, when there is available to us a system of rule that is not of this world. God's order for mankind was always different. Ever since the whole world came under Satan's rule when mankind fell into sin, we have operated under Satan's kingdom's rule. Jesus brought back His Kingdom to earth. God's kingdom rule is to be the order of God's people.

Prayer:

Lord, is there a way that I am abusing power? I know I can't live fully in Your power if that is so. Help me to see power from Your perspective and not my own. Make me comfortable being clothed in Your power. Teach me how to use Your power on the unseen enemies. Thank You for a new beginning.

CHAPTER 16

Women and Power

"Be strong in the Lord, and in the power of His might."
Ephesians 6:10

AS THE SAYING GOES, THE HAND that rocks the cradle rules the world. Everyone is related to a woman, because everyone has a mother. And mothers have an enormous power of influence. Government officials and successful business executives have mothers who tell them what to do, just like everyone else.

A friend of mine, who recently wrote a book, was thinking about calling a local talk show about an appearance to publicize her book, but had not yet done so. She had the opportunity to meet a woman who had read her book, and when she spoke with this woman, she was told to call the talk show and tell the host that his *mother* said he should have this author on his show. Even after children are grown and have children of their own, even grandchildren of their own, mothers sometimes tell them what to do.

The power of influence
From the beginning of a child's life, women have the power to shape character through their encouragement and teaching. Women can determine destinies by using their power to motivate children to excellence. Many people have risen to greatness because a mother or a teacher told them they could do it. A 1996 *Newsweek* article spoke of the value both the current President of the United States, Bill Clinton, and the man who ran to get his job, Bob Dole, placed on their now-deceased mothers. Think of all the sports stars who wave to or thank their moms at every opportunity.

Not only do women hold influence over children, but they can use their favor with God to obtain answers from Him for themselves and others in their lives. When Jesus walked the earth, many women came to Him on behalf of their loved ones. The Syrophoenician woman begged Jesus to cast the demon out of her daughter (Mark 7:26). Martha and Mary came to Jesus on behalf of their brother, Lazarus (John 11). I imagine many of the people who brought their infants to Jesus (Luke 18:15) were women. Today, many women go to their heavenly Father in prayer on behalf of the needs of their family members. Just as Hannah gave her son Samuel to the service of the Lord, women today give their children to God's service by dedicating them to the Lord as infants.

Women set the tone in our homes, communities, and churches. Have you ever gone into a house and sensed an atmosphere of peace—or conflict? In all likelihood a woman was responsible for it. If you have a female boss, you can readily tell by her mood on Monday morning how her weekend went. A woman's mood pervades her surroundings.

It has been said, "Behind every successful man is a woman." That is true. The woman, however, may not be a wife. It may be a mother, a sister, an aunt, a grandmother, even a teacher or a neighbor.

It is important for women to understand the power bestowed on them. When we do not understand power, we abuse what we have through neglect or misuse; or we try to obtain powers that have nothing to do with our unique design and purpose. Women who know their purpose and have an intimate knowledge of working in unity with their God can use the power God has given to command thought, opinion, and behavior in their own minds, souls, and bodies. We can have the power to be keys to change in our families, churches, and communities.

The God-given power of influence has the potential to change human hearts. The power of influence could really rule the world.

Influence causes a person to do something they know they should not do, or even to do something they do not really want to do. It can be applied to either good and bad ends. It's the power with which Eve influenced Adam to eat the forbidden fruit. It's the power with which Abigail convinced David not to murder her husband. It's the power Eunice and Lois used to train Timothy. It's the power Phoebe had as a helper to Paul.

The power of influence has its origin in the very wisdom of God. It's how Deborah knew what to do to defeat the enemy. It's why the leaders followed her advice. She had heard from God, because she had a relationship of intimacy with God. It did not matter that she was a woman. She was God's spokesperson for the hour. (Aren't you glad God does not discriminate with whom He is intimate?)

I believe the power of influence is the second greatest power available. It is the power that changes things unseen. It is a ruling power. The difference between the power of influence and the power of authority is that the power of influence changes *hearts*, not just outward actions.

A woman's power of influence has not always been fully appreciated. Women have so many opportunities to use this power. It is so vitally important that our enemy would often have us despise that power and strive for other powers. Women have power that will bring about *real* change. In many ways, it is power that we have been tricked into neglecting—or worse, abusing.

We women often use the power of influence when we want our own way. Men have robbed, killed, and even waged wars in order to please a woman or to get her something she wanted. On the other hand, wars and fights have been aborted because a woman intervened. Think of what could happen if thousands of women who desire to see the ways of God reign, used their power of influence to promote righteousness, peace, unity, and the love of God.

Understanding the awesome power of influence would make us much more comfortable in our purpose as demonstrators of Spirit living. When we add to the power of influence the ability to use the power of loving service, as I alluded to earlier, we become close partners with God. In that junior partnership relationship with God, we can exercise the power of control under God's auspices and direction. Let me also be clear that we will always be in a *junior* partnership with God. We don't get to be God. God alone is God. However, His Spirit is in us. We are His daughters. We get to do God's works as He directs and leads us.

Power of loving service

Ministry means service. We touched on the related powers of control and authority. We've covered the power of influence. Now, let's cover the last power, which really comes first. The power of loving service was ordained by God for the ruling of His people, the Body of Christ, the church, not as an organization, but as an organism. The leadership of God's church is structured completely opposite to the world system. The church was never meant to operate under the hierarchical system imported from hell. God's Kingdom is sometimes called the upside-down kingdom, because everything is done so differently from the way the world does things. Jesus had a leadership style that was revolutionary. To Him, leadership meant servanthood.

In *The Jesus Style,* Gayle Erwin says this about servanthood power:

> For reasons I cannot understand, I have not, in my research, found the qualities of servanthood, which seem so self-evident and basic to who Jesus is, treated in any but a surface and brief way. I only know that the realization of them and even minimal

incorporation of them into life has power that I cannot de
scribe...[1]

We have two systems of operation. One is the Kingdom of
God's system led by the King of Kings, Jesus Christ. The other is
the world system led by Satan. In the last chapter we already
considered the world's hierarchical system of order. We do little
to advance the Kingdom of God if we try to use the methods of
the system. That's why Jesus was so explicit about the difference
between His Kingdom and the way the world does things.

It is obvious to me that the Christian religion of "Churchianity," has gotten caught up in the wrong system. There are
many books in Christian bookstores about being a success in
ministry, increasing the size of your church, church management,
setting goals, etc. There are few books about servant leadership.
Two that I recommend are *Improving Your Serve* by Chuck Swindoll
and *The Jesus Style* by Gayle Erwin. Swindoll, in *Improving Your Serve*,
has this to say on the current state of affairs in today's churches:

> In the secular system there are distinct levels of authority. It's
> true today, for sure. . . . the boss is in charge. That is the way the
> system works. As Jesus put it, "their great men exercise authority
> over them." But then he adds, "It is *not so* among you" (emphasis
> added). What isn't so? Simply this, in God's family there is to be
> one great body of people: servants. In fact, that's the way to the
> top in His kingdom . . . "whoever wishes to become great among
> you shall be your servant."

Yes, these seem to be forgotten words, even in many churches
with their smooth pastors, high powered executives, and super-
star singers. Unfortunately, there doesn't seem to be much of
the servant mentality in such settings. Even in our church life
we tend to get so caught up in a success and size race that we lose
sight of our primary calling as followers of Christ. The "celebrity

syndrome" so present in our Christian thought and activities just doesn't square with the attitudes and messages of Jesus. We have skidded into a pattern whereby the celebrities and top dogs in our church life call the shots, and it is difficult to be a servant when you're used to telling others what to do.[2]

In *The Jesus Style*, Erwin has this to say on church authority structures:

"Rulers of the Gentiles Lord it over... Not so with you. It amazes me how many of our church and religious systems break apart when analyzed in terms of this command, and yet we continue claiming our structure to be biblical and authorized of God.

The principle of being servant to all is devastating to chains of command and to systems where submission is upward. Many religious structures are carbon copies of the flow-charts of giant corporations where the "lording" system is pyramid shaped. In the kingdom of God, the power pyramid is reversed, up-ended, so that the authority is on the bottom, not the top.

When Jesus alludes to submission, it is always directed towards leaders or the ones who want to be great in the kingdom and they are always ordered to submit downward, not upward. . . .

. . . We lord it over others because we don't recognize their value and don't view them in the way Jesus does.[3]

Jesus expanded this concept of servant leadership when He denounced the scribes and Pharisees by denouncing the current religious system, Jesus was describing what His system was *not*. In the middle of His discourse recorded in Matthew 23, He drops in what His kingdom is all about. He tells the religious leaders how to be great in God's Kingdom.

But be not ye called Rabbi: for one is your Master, even Christ; and all ye are brethren. And call no man your father upon the earth: for one is your Father, which is in heaven. Neither be ye called masters: for one is your Master, even Christ. But he that is greatest among you shall be your servant. And whosoever shall exalt himself shall be abased; and he that shall humble himself shall be exalted. (Matthew 23:1-15 & 23-34).

Gayle Erwin goes on to say:

There are so many ways that the nature of Jesus is in direct opposition to the leadership patterns of the world that have been unquestioningly adopted by the church. We have been so careful to identify doctrinal heresy; perhaps it is time to identify heresy of practice. [4]

Servant leadership has love as its goal. Servant leadership, or loving service, is based on putting oneself down beneath others to hold them up. It's not about lording it over others. It's not about superiority and inferiority. It's about counting everyone worthy of value. Even if the one called to servant leadership is more knowledgeable or more gifted than those he (or she) is serving, he makes himself of no reputation. He esteems others better than himself. He does not think he is God's gift to everyone else. He does not put himself in a position where he is unaccountable to others. He acknowledges his need for others.

The Apostle Paul gave a great description of servant leadership when he wrote the Philippian church about Jesus' style of leadership:

Let nothing be done through strife or vainglory; but in lowliness of mind let each esteem others better than themselves. Look not every man on his own things, but every man also on the things of others. Let this mind be in you, which was also in Christ Jesus: Who, being in the form of God, thought it not robbery to be equal with God: But made himself of no reputation, and took upon him the form of a servant, and was made in the likeness of men: And being found in fashion as a man, he humbled himself, and became obedient unto death, even the death of the cross. Wherefore God also hath highly exalted him, and given him a name which is above every name. (Philippians 2:3-9)

Love is a powerful force. Love is the way of the kingdom of God. Spirit living is walking in the agape love that comes only from God. Clearly, the world's system of striving, control, manipulation, coercion, lust, and pride (1 John 2:15) does not mix with God's system. Frustration and burnout are evident in those people and institutions who try to mix the two systems. Effective servant leaders understand this key principle.

What can we do?

I'm not sure what you and I can do about the state of affairs of the church. Certainly, all of us need to pray that God's kingdom and God's will be done in His own Body. And, if we are truly called to minister to the people in His Body, we would do well to pattern ourselves after Jesus' style of service and not what has been adapted from the world system.

Women, we can get on and do the work of the kingdom, forgetting jockeying for position and power among men. Or we can get caught up in the world's system and spin our wheels striving for what looks good, but is going nowhere. The choice is ours.

One thing is sure: if we want to move on up to Spirit living, we have to seek a different power base. That power base is loving service. It doesn't make a lot of sense, based on what we observe in this world and even in our churches, but it is biblical.

The servant leadership style must permeate all our relationships. It is not just for those in active service or ministry. We need to use it in our homes, our jobs, and our communities, as well as in our churches. The power of love does not destroy a person's will in order to get him to comply. It reaches to the demonic strongholds behind that unlovable child in your classroom. It recognizes that unruly child as created in the image of God, and loves him in spite of his actions. This power is available only in direct connection to God. It draws on the *agape* love of God.

We have touched on the power available to women. It is important to know about this, because when women walk in spiritual power, change will be inevitable. The goal of this book is to guide women into proper connection with the ultimate power Source, so that we use our God-given powers in a manner to bring about the change God wants to see.

Prayer:

Father, you have given me a lot of power. I have not always recognized how much You have trusted me. I have not always used this power in godly ways. Please forgive me. Thank You for giving me this opportunity to be a partner with You in a power that will make a difference in this world.

CHAPTER 17

Words: The Power Tools

"A wholesome tongue is a tree of life."

Proverbs 15:4

IN THE BEGINNING GOD CREATED the heavens and the earth. Something mysterious happened between Genesis 1:1 and Genesis 1:2, because the second verse says that after God created the earth, it became formless and empty ("the earth was without form and void . . ."). What could have happened to turn order into chaos? Thankfully, ". . . then God, by the power of the Holy Spirit, began to move upon the face of the deep." (Genesis 1:2a)

After that, God used words. He *spoke* creation into existence, and a new beginning and new life came forth. Words were the power tools God used for creation. Words are the power tools women who have moved beyond religion to Spirit living will use to bring new life to chaotic situations.

Since the very beginning, God has had good plans for our lives, and for the lives of our loved ones. Something happened to bring a void, a lack of purpose, into our lives. God still wants to move upon those empty spaces. God uses words to bring back His good plans. Women can be partners with God by speaking God-filled words over the voids in their own lives, as well as the voids in the lives of loved ones, family members, and acquaintances. God gave us His Word and His instruction on how we are to use our tongues to honor Him.

Words have creative power

Words are instruments of power and of life. God used words to bring life into existence. God upholds the world now by the Word of His power (Hebrews 1:3). In Genesis, we see how the world was formed when God spoke. Everything we see came from the spoken word of God. Jesus declared He was the Word of Life. The book of John tells us that Jesus was there in the beginning.

> In the beginning was the Word, and the Word was with God, and the Word was God. The same was in the beginning with God. All things were made by him; and without him was not any thing made that was made. In him was life; and the life was the light of men. And the light shineth in darkness; and the darkness comprehended it not. (John 1:1-5)

We saw that women can exercise the powers of loving service, influence, and authority over unclean spirits. As we grow in the Word and in the Spirit, we have the power, under God, to use the Word of God as containers of God's creative power of control.

God used words beyond creation. Throughout the Word of God, words are used as spiritual weapons (Jeremiah 47:6,7; 55:11; Isaiah 11:4; Jeremiah 23:28, 29; 2 Thessalonians 2:8). Jesus defeated the Devil's plan of temptation with words (Luke 4:2-13). In the Apostle John's vision, Jesus uses a two-edged sword out of his mouth to bring final defeat to Satan (Revelation 19:15).

God also uses words for healing: "He sent his Word and healed them" (Psalm 107:20). Jesus used words to heal people physically and spiritually. He said to the woman who had a spirit of infirmity for eighteen years, "Woman, thou art loosed from thine infirmity" (Luke 13:12). He said to blind Bartimaeus, "Go thy way; thy faith hath made thee whole" (Mark 10:52).

Jesus even spoke to a storm at sea and brought calm (Mark 4:39). Words can and will change people and circumstances. Jesus, said, "It is the spirit that quickeneth; the flesh profiteth nothing: the words that I speak unto you, they are spirit, and they are life" (John 6:63).

Women and the importance of words

Genesis tells us that mankind is made in the image of God (Genesis 1:26). God uses words, so it follows that His image bearers use words. Words have a powerful place in the lives of most women. When a woman is properly connected to God, walking in God's power, God can use her words to bring new life and new beginnings into empty, dead-end situations.

God has granted women the creative powers to use spoken words to reverse the curses on our families. The proper use of words by someone whose life demonstrates a Spirit-filled walk will indeed bring about change. We can go to God in prayer for ourselves, our sisters, and others. As we bring prayers to God, and allow His encouragement and blessing to flow from our lips, our tongues will become fountains of life.

I believe women can obtain the power to use their words to change actual situations and people if we're willing to go through what it takes to be in a close relationship with God.

Let me emphasize, the power is not in people going around speaking what they want into existence when they are not close to God. God, in His mercy, may give a few baby or carnal Christians some of the things they have confessed to keep them encouraged until they grow up. On the other hand, Satan can also manipulate situations through our words. That's why it's very important to watch the words we speak. We could put curses on people that our enemy is only too happy to carry out.

Christian women have been given a purpose to be partners with God in bringing spiritual life to the body of Christ. It is essential that we grow in God, so that His Spirit is our life source, not "religion" or our own strength. When we have the fullness of God's Spirit operating in our lives, the words which come out of our mouths will cease to be a mixture of blessings and curses, and we will speak words only to bless.

A Fountain of Life

Encouragement
- "You can do it."
- "It will be all right."
- "God will see you through."
- "God will do great things through you."

Blessing
- "You're wonderful."
- "I like your honesty."
- "You're really talented."
- "You did a great job."
- "You did your best."

Just as women are physically designed to conceive, bring forth, and nurture life in the natural realm, women also can conceive, bring forth, and nurture life in the spiritual realm. According to the Scripture, spiritual life flows through the tongue: "Life is in the power of the tongue" (Proverbs 18:21).

Life through words

There is power in encouraging words. A simple word of encouragement can make or break a person. Sometimes we don't curse people with actual words, but by neglecting to say something encouraging. In the act of withholding encouragement, we sin. Knowing the right thing to do, but neglecting to act on that knowledge is sin (James 4:17).

A woman's words can bring hope, peace, healing, and strength to others. Probably every woman reading this book can think of a critical time in her life when God used the words of another to bring comfort and peace. I can remember a time, right before a dear friend of mine died from breast cancer, when I received phone calls from two friends, both of whom told me that I had been very heavily on their minds. They had prayed for me first, then called to find out what was going on in my life. I had no idea my friend was going to die that week, but the words and prayers of those two women were a real comfort to me when her death came to pass. I remember thinking, "God, you knew I was going to face difficulty this week, and you already had people praying for me before I could ask for it."

My friends used their words with wisdom. They prayed first. Then they called and encouraged me. When God brings people to our minds, let's not neglect to pray for them. Many African American women are full of heartache and are living in pain and stress. We can be of great encouragement to each other by our words. Ask God to help you encourage someone today.

The change that has to come

Before we can use words properly, our hearts have to change. Before the Word in our mouth is powerful and effective, the Word has to work on us, dividing our soul from our spirit (Hebrews 4:12).

We have seen that change is not easy. Nor is it easy to admit the need for change. But it wasn't easy staying where we were, either. God would never trust His true power tools to those who do not live in Him. God wants to take the life He has placed in our spirit and bring it to our tongues and then to the ears of others. A wholesome tongue is a tree of life (Proverbs 15:4).

God has designed us to be living, or spirit/souls. It is in the spiritual realm that we begin to fulfill our destiny. Unbelievers have no choice but to live out of their souls. The believer has a choice to live either out of her spirit or out of her soul. We have already seen the difference between our souls and our human spirits in the chapter on the heart/tongue connection. Our use of words will change as we begin to understand how to live by the power of our spirit, empowered by God's Holy Spirit. This understanding is crucial in fulfilling our purposes and to rightly using the power tools God has given us as women. As we stated earlier, maturity in the Spirit does not come without a taming of the tongue. Our tongues are tamed as our hearts are healed.

"The words of a man's mouth are as deep waters" (Proverbs 18:4). We have the privilege to join with the Lord in bringing new life to the situations and circumstances of our lives. We share in God's power to speak life into existence. Words are the containers of spiritual power that God has given us, His partners.

Using words, a woman fulfills her spiritual purpose. If we learn to use words properly, our own lives will change, our families will change, our churches will change, and our communities will change. Women play key roles in their households and families. Their influence is felt in the collection of households we call a neighborhood, in the group of neighborhoods that make up a city, and in the many cities that comprise a nation.

Grace upon us and through us

The grace of God changes our lives. If we are saved, we may go boldly to the throne of grace and ask God to impart that same grace to others (Hebrews 4:16). Our words are seasoned with grace, and that grace flows to others through our speech. By God's grace, we become instruments of God's grace (Ephesians 4:29).

It's through the wise use of words that women can influence the world for good. With our tongues, we can encourage others to greatness, to betterment, to excellence. With our tongues, we can tell young people, "You can make it."

A woman's key input into the lives of children comes in the form of words. With one's own children and with nephews, nieces, neighborhood children, or students in a classroom, words need to be used liberally to encourage children, to bless them, and to speak good destinies for them. Many people can point back to someone—a teacher, aunt, mother, or neighbor—whose words helped them consider college or a career that they had not thought they were capable of pursuing. Others know that someone's words kept them from giving up on life.

I will never forget a Christian teacher who encouraged me to hold my head up when I was ashamed of my height. When I began to write, God used Margaret Sebastian, a friend whose words are always so encouraging, to keep me going. I did not believe in myself, but her words helped me see that perhaps others could be helped by what I had to say.

We should look daily for opportunities to encourage others, especially the children whom God has placed in our lives. For those who have no children of their own, God may want to use you to speak in the lives of nephews, nieces, and neighborhood children. Sometimes, mothering can be so tiring that mothers neglect to give these gifts of life to their own children. Mothers need encouragement. Let us not neglect to bring words of encouragement to them and to all the children who cross our paths.

A woman who knows her purpose and power is a woman aware of her destiny, alert to assignments in her home, church, community, or workplace. She knows her purpose is to bring life. She will be on the lookout for death and darkness, knowing that she can help bring life into the dark places of our families, neighborhoods, and cities.

Words have creative power. Let your words create divine change. "He quickens the dead and calls those things that are not as though they were" (Romans 4:17). "He upholds all things by the word of his power" (Hebrews 1:3). Your words will not return void if they are spoken from His mouth (Isaiah 55:11).

In summary, spiritual power has been given to women to reverse the curse on our families. Words are the power tools in our arsenal as we seek to lovingly serve. God will use us as agents of change because we have yielded our tongues to Him.

Prayer:

Lord, I need an abundant outpouring of your grace in my life today and every day. Take away the feelings of despair and hopelessness. Let the words of my mouth and the meditations of my heart be acceptable in your sight. Help me to be an encouragement to others. Teach me to talk to you in prayer more than I talk to others and more than I talk to myself.

CHAPTER 18

Movin' On Up in Service

"I will pour out of my Spirit upon all flesh: . . . on my handmaidens I will pour out in those days of my Spirit; and they shall prophesy."

Acts 2:17-18.

I BELIEVE WE WOULD SEE MUCH more accomplished for change if the ability of women to demonstrate spiritual life was emphasized more in our churches. It is fundamental to a woman's ministry. But are there times when women are also called to speak to men? Is all of our ministry to be limited to demonstrating spiritual life and/or to prayer?

I believe God is raising up an army of women who will go into enemy territory to tear down strongholds. They will burst down the prison gates to bring out the millions of people trapped by the enemy in immorality, violence, anger, addictions, and institutionalized religions such as Islam and Churchianity. This army of women will take their places beside men.

These women warriors are called to serve in God's Kingdom. They have moved beyond religion to Spirit living for a purpose. They are women in ministry—serving the King and bringing from His throne room service to others.

In the Spirit, there is no male or female (Galatians 3:28). The purposes of women in God's Body have both natural and spiritual implications. Though there is no difference between males and females in the Spirit, when we are in natural relationships with each other, there are some things that are unique to men and some things unique to women. My examination of the Scriptures shows that in natural relationships between men and women, men are most often in headship or visible leadership roles. But don't let that trouble you or make you think less of yourself. Women can have leadership roles in the Spirit that are second to none.

What is ministry?
Every person who is a part of the family of God is called to be in ministry. God's purpose for some people is to equip others for the work of the ministry. Those who have this responsibility and form of ministry are not more important than others, nor less accountable. They should not set themselves above others, and should not try to replace God in the lives of others. Rather, they must carry out their responsibility, serving from beneath rather than above. Their mission is to work themselves out of a job.

The service one does for the people of God is either to minister life to those in the Body or to train others to minister life. Body life ministry and equipping ministry are two different things. When we confuse the two, we harm the whole Body. It is important for each of us to know our place in the Body as members who need each other. We also need to know whether or not we are called to operate in an equipping ministry, and if so, we need to learn how to perform that role with the proper servant attitude.

Everybody needs to receive body life ministry from others. That has nothing to do with a person's role as an equipping minister. People in equipping roles need body life from members of the Body, not necessarily just from others who have equipping ministries. God has set up the Body in such a way that we need each other on a daily basis (Acts 2:46; Ephesians 4:16). No one is allowed to say "because you are not a mouth, arm, or hand like me, I have no need of you" (1 Corinthians 12:21). This is how it is in God's blueprint. The distinction between clergy and laity is part of the erroneous blueprint that has been substituted for God's true plans for the church.

Body life is encouraging and admonishing one another according to the Scripture. Body life ministry is essential to Christian maturity and Spirit living. We are admonished to encourage one another, pray for one another, provoke one another to good works, and confess our faults one to another. There are many other forms of body life ministry we are to do to and with one another. None of these can be done sitting in a pew looking at a platform and the back of someone's head.

Body life ministry as described in Scripture, has been factored out of the church structure since about A.D. 300, when the church became a political institution. Before A.D. 300, the majority of what took place among members in the body of Christ in any one locality was body life. I personally believe that a good three-fourths of what should be going on when Christians get together should be the members of the Body expressing ministry to each other. The other one-fourth of the time we come together we can worship in a corporate fashion and receive teaching or some other form of equipping ministry.

Church life before A.D. 300 took place in home setting small enough for one-on-one ministry. It was not mass production churning out hundreds of cookie-cutter Christians. Church buildings as we know them today were not necessary back then because large numbers were not the goal. House church meetings were the strength of the early Church. People were accountable to one another for their lives as Christians. Everybody came prepared to participate and contribute to the life of the Body (1 Corinthians 14:16). Each person was considered a priest of God, able to hear Him and also to speak for Him. People did not hire others to do ministry to them or to hear from God for them. When the saints came together, ministry was not left up to one person!

After a few years just sitting under teaching with no outlet, most people stagnate. When people get full and haven't been able to exercise what God has given them among the other people of God, the tendency is to try to find an outlet. When people called to minister body life to the saints—that's all of us—have little opportunity to do so when the Body comes together, they too often feel that they must start another church in order to do ministry.

Now, I'm all for new churches. The natural process of growth is division. When a group of people grow too big, they can divide into two smaller groups. Smaller often is better for the growth of individuals. What saddens me is that division too often is forced because of a lack of opportunity to do body ministry. This is not a good foundation for ministry, especially when this takes place with bitterness, competition, or animosity, which is often the case.

Equipping ministry

We have noted that everyone is called to body life ministry. We have also said that some are called to equipping ministries. There are five equipping ministries listed in Ephesians 4:16: apostle, prophet, evangelist, pastor or teacher. All five were given to bring maturity to the body. All five are needed to bring balance. Are women called to these equipping roles in the Body of Christ?

The major problem is not the gender of those in equipping ministries, but the system under which equipping ministers currently operate. There are needs and hurts that are being overlooked under the current ministry system. Most of that neglect would be alleviated if body life ministry were emphasized over equipping ministry.

However, I believe women are indeed called to equipping ministries to fill this void. That's why conferences among women are so popular. Women are coming together to learn from women about issues facing them that are often neglected in the church setting.

Are women called to be pastors? If you define "pastor" in the role we currently see, I do not think women are called to those positions. Frankly, I don't think men are called to those positions either, at least not in the sense of a traditional pastor who is "apart" from his congregation and whose authority is unquestioned. But yes, if you define "pastor" as "shepherd" as one who disciples a few people, the way Jesus discipled twelve; one who heals broken hearts, one who keeps the wolves away, and leads sheep to green pastures (teachings). I believe a woman can fill that role in the life of others in the Body, especially other women.

The shepherding role necessitates a small group setting. Someone who is shepherding another in the biblical sense of the word has to come close enough to be able to be a bishop or overseer of the other person's soul—mind, will, and emotions (1 Peter 2:25). Paul took others under his wing as he traveled on his missionary journeys. This was part of his pastoring/mentoring work.

A small group setting in not needed for other forms of equipping ministry other than pastoral. Most of Paul's apostolic, prophetic, and teaching work as a master builder, laying the foundation for the people of God was accomplished through letters. The avenues available today—books, newsletters, tapes, conferences, seminars, television, and radio—afford us the opportunity to do equipping ministry on many different levels.

Women ministering to men

Paul's words to Timothy that he "does not permit a woman to teach a man" (2 Timothy 2:12) raise many questions. When I had trouble believing God was calling me to ministry, I read some of the arguments that explain how this scripture can be interpreted in the light of other passages of the Bible that clearly show women in ministry to men. Anyone who feels a call to teach men should have enough basis to proceed. To be honest with you, I personally still have reservations, but at the same time, I do not question another person's call. If you are interested in exploring the arguments that allow women to teach men take a look at *Women in the Church: A Biblical Theology in Ministry* by Stanley J. Grenz with Denise Kjesb (IVP), *Who Said Women Can't Teach?* by Charles Tromball (Logos

Books), and *Women in Ministry* by L. E. Maywell with Ruth C. Deoring (Victor Books).

In all fairness, there are a number of arguments on the other side of the fence which prohibit women from teaching men. Sometimes its hard to sort through tradition, sexism, and Scripture. I have not seen an argument that was free from all of that. One book that came the closest is *Biblical Eldership: An Urgent Call To Restore Biblical Church Leadership* by Alexander Stauch (Lewis And Roth Publishers).

No matter what your conviction on women teaching men, a couple of things from Scripture are clear to me: (1) men more often have roles of visible leadership; (2) visible roles of leadership have little to do with authority in the spirit realm; (3) visibility would ruin some of God's most strategic plans for advancement into the enemy's kingdom; (4) submission is important for everyone, but even more important for women because being under authority gives us greater authority in the spirit world; (5) a woman should not be in a role of authority over her own husband.

Though I am open to the possibility that God may call a few women to teach men; because of the background in which I was raised, I am uncomfortable teaching men myself. Consequently, I do not have a problem refraining from teaching men. The way I see it, the church population is made up mostly of women anyway—so what if my ministry is restricted to women? I believe I have a message that speaks uniquely to women. The Bible clearly instructs women to teach women (Titus 2:4). I have more than enough ministry if I limit myself to women only.

Even though most of what I teach is largely for women, I think men—whether or not they are pastors—have a right and responsibility to hear what I am teaching their parishioners, wives, sisters, and daughters. If the Holy Spirit teaches them something through me in the process, so be it. There is a difference between *teaching* and *speaking*. No matter what one believes about whether or not a women can *teach* men, I don't think God is above using a woman to *speak* when men are present.

It is abundantly clear in the Word of God that women can pray and speak words of prophecy in the presence of men (1 Corinthians 11:5). To prophesy means to edify, exhort, or comfort. Prophetic words are meant to minister to the hearers. They are words that God will give a woman to say which will speak to both men and women.

Jesus told the women at the tomb to proclaim to the disciples that He had risen from the dead. If it was a disgrace for men to receive a message from the mouths of women, Jesus would not have asked women to carry the most important message ever given anyone to carry. He easily could have appeared to the disciples personally, or He could have waited until one of the men came to the empty tomb himself.

Paul speaks of the many women—including Junia, who was referred to as an apostle—who were co-laborers with him in the work of the ministry (Romans 16:1-7). It is clear that Paul received the body life ministry of many women in his personal life. It is also likely he received equipping ministry from female peers.

Anna was a prophetess (Luke 2:36). Philip, the evangelist, had four daughters who prophesied (Acts 21:8). Priscilla, along with her husband, Aquilla, was used of God to instruct Apollos in "the way more perfect" (Acts 18:26). Obviously, God uses women to speak to men. God retains the right to use even a donkey. Surely, women are more valued than donkeys!

The Old Testament

The role of a prophet or prophetess in the Old Testament was to speak for God to the people of Israel. We have the example of Miriam, who was a prophetess. She was also listed as one that God used along with her two brothers, Moses and Aaron (Micah 6:4) to bring the people of Israel out of Egypt. Huldah (2 Kings 22:14), Noadiah (Nehemiah 6:14), and Isaiah's wife (Isaiah 8:3) also were prophetesses.

Deborah, a judge of Israel, challenged an Israelite general, Barak, to do what the Lord had already instructed him to do. If you remember the story, Barak wouldn't do what God had told him to do on his own. He was only willing to do it if Deborah went with him (Judges 4:4-9). Just as an Old Testament prophet's or prophetess' job was to speak for the Lord to Israel, in the New Testament God also used prophets and prophetesses to speak to His people.

Now that we've established that God wants to use in service the woman who has moved on up to live with Him in the Spirit, let's take a peek at how that ministry might look.

Prayer:
Father, Please clarify the ministry you have called me to. I am willing to lay on the altar any preconceived ideas of what it all means. Please show me the new thing that You want to do. Let me be a part of the new ministry team You are building. I'm ready to go to battle for You.

CHAPTER 19

Movin' to a New Pattern

"No man putteth new wine into old bottles: else the new
wine doth burst the bottles, and the wine is spilled . . .
but new wine must be put into new bottles."

Mark 2:22

FOR MANY YEARS, GOD USED ME behind the scenes in a
prayer ministry. I had done a little speaking in Chicago.
Working as a nurse in the field of addiction, I learned a lot about
broken and attached hearts. When I moved to Detroit, most of my
teaching and speaking was in this field. Except for a few occasions,
I had been put on a shelf from speaking for a few years. While I
was writing *Chosen Vessels*, I was involved with three different small
prayer groups. At the one that met early Saturday mornings, I also
did some instructing. The women there, Bridgett, Evelyn, Deme-
tyre, Lynette, and Linda were a real source of encouragement to
me at that time. Some of the material I used was the basis of *Chosen
Vessels*.

After *Chosen Vessels* came out, I began to speak again. So at
this time, God is using me in public teaching and speaking, as well
as writing and prayer ministry. I have accepted the public ministry
because it is what God wants at this time; but, to be truthful, I
would rather be where I started out, in the prayer closet, where
nobody knew my name. I find that though I still have a call to pray
and seek to fulfill that along with the new ministry, if it weren't for
the training in the prayer closet, I would not be able to handle the
present ministry.

I enjoy meeting God's chosen vessels. I enjoy bringing God's
Word to women. I appreciate the kindness I receive when I travel
to different places. Seeing new places can be exciting. But the
highlight of last year was teaching two classes on intercessory prayer

to a few women in my living room. I can go somewhere for a weekend and share with up to three hundred women and trust that lives are changed. But it's more exciting when I can see the change week to week. I'm more convinced than ever that we need to take a closer look at the ministry God esteems important.

I believe everyone's first ministry is speaking with God. Even the apostles realized the importance of prayer, and they tried to have some free time to spend in prayer and the ministry of the Word (Acts 6:4). Prayer was their first priority. You have to minister to God before you have anything to minister to people. According to a specific survey, the average length of time pastors pray is 22 minutes per day. Some pray as few as 7 minutes per day.[1]

What are you going to give others if you do not spend time in the presence of God? How can you minister life and model Spirit living if you do not spend adequate time with the Master? I'm talking about more than just reading the Bible everyday. I'm talking about letting the Bible read you. I'm talking about taking days, even weeks, to fast and get alone with the Lord in prayer, letting Him deal with your fears, insecurities, and disobedience. We have to spend undistracted time with God to get His strategies for our families, communities, and churches.

It's tempting for those called into ministry to get caught up in administrative duties, programs, activities, and going before the people. Before we know it, it'll be the people we'll fear and not God. We will obey them and not God. We'll give the people what they want to hear and we will not tell them what God tells us to say. We may be popular and we may be prosperous, but at what price? We may not get to hear Him say, "Well done, thou good and faithful servant."

It does not take a lot of spirituality to have a ministry speaking to people. If you have some oratorical skills and can learn from others by reading or listening, you can find something to say to people. Your words may not necessarily change people's lives, but people will like you and tell you you've done a fine job. They'll invite you different places to speak. It takes more spiritual maturity to have a ministry in the prayer closet than it takes to have a ministry with people.

The prayer closet is a place of intimacy with God. In there, I must face myself in all my nakedness. I can hide from people what I cannot hide from God. If I had gone into ministry to people without that prayer ministry with God in the hidden places, the impact of my speaking would be very limited. God can and will use women beyond demonstrating spiritual life, and in addition to prayer. But, first let's get our equipping in the prayer closet, and our credentials in the ability to demonstrate spiritual life.

The waiting room

I mentioned in an earlier chapter that I had some serious problems accepting what I felt was God's call into ministry. Once I accepted the call, I had a lot of problems waiting for its fulfillment. As I have met women across the United States, I have noticed that many of them have also experienced a call on their lives. They too, experience impatience, frustration, doubt and many questions. The most important thing I can say about the waiting room is: You don't have to wait to minister. Forget about what has been defined as ministry, and work right where you are. I realize that might not encompass all you have sensed God has given you to do. That's okay. That fulfillment will come to pass at its proper time. You cannot make it happen.

As I look back, I now see that I was ministering all the time I was waiting for the doors to open, frustrated that God was not cooperating. "God called me," I would say. "Why didn't He tell those in leadership that I was called?" Yet I was ministering. I was ministering when I volunteered at the youth home while I was in college. I was ministering when the Lord led me to disciple the newborn Christian on my job, and when I joined my husband in his hospital visitation ministry in Chicago. I was ministering by spending time with my family. I served words of encouragement many times over the phone, even a few times through the mail.

It should go without saying that a married woman's first ministry is in her home. But it needs to be said. If God has not worked in your husband's heart to the point that he is ready to release you, it's probably not time yet. Believe me, if you have a true call of God on your life, Satan will tempt you to neglect your family or friends for the sake of all the people who need you.

If you're still worried about when and how, it's not time yet. I believe God's best comes when you have totally given up all hope. When you have ceased from trying to make it happen and when you don't even care when, God will bring it to pass. Of course, you can waste a lot of time birthing Ishmaels, but God won't be in them.

Ministry flows from intimacy

Prayer is the key to ministry. Prayer definitely is a calling for women, as we have noted before. As much as humans esteem those who preach and teach, God esteems those who are intimate with Him and can get a prayer through.

God calls everyone to intimacy with Himself. Ministry to others flows out of that intimacy. I wonder how much of what is called ministry today is actually an overflow of intimacy with God. Women do the Body of Christ a disservice if they pattern their ministry after what they have seen demonstrated.

We have teachings and sermons in abundance in this country. But they haven't closed the crack houses down. Yet, I did hear that a town in Massachusetts pinpointed prayer as the means that shut crack houses down there. They were losing their children to crack, so people of different denominations joined together to go to the streets, one block at a time, to pray for the crack houses to be closed. After about a year, each of the houses they had prayed over was no longer a crack house. Prayer and revival are credited for drastic social changes in other cities, as well. Let's get back to the real work of the church: prayer.

The great switch

Today's patterns of ministries were not established by God. I am convinced that the reason the Body of Christ has been unable to recapture the effectiveness of the early Church is that the blueprint for the structure of the church got switched around A.D.300.

About A.D. 300 a Roman emperor named Constantine, supposedly had a conversion experience. This was during the time when the Christians were being persecuted. He stopped the persecution of Christians. He also thought he was doing the Christians a big favor by making Christianity the state religion. He felt the church needed priests, like all the pagan religions. In fact, he took most of what was going on in pagan religions and put it in the Christian Church. He decided that the intimacy of home churches was not good enough for this new state religion, so he subsidized the building of church buildings where Christians could go once a week.[2]

The place of the Word of God in the life of individuals was no longer the same. The priests were now caretakers of the Word. The congregation got what was feed to them by the priest. The Church has never fully recovered from the devastating blow given it by Constantine's "favor." Saints such as Martin Luther dot our historical landscape with renewal, but we've never regained the vigor and vitality of that early Church.

Before A.D. 300, people who loved God with all their hearts and who had given their lives in full commitment to God were a serious threat to Satan's kingdom. The Church of the first and second centuries made major advances against the kingdom of darkness. People's lives were changed. Cities were turned right side up. Satan tried persecution to stop the advances into his kingdom, but that only made things worse for him. When he saw the Church continuing to make advances into his kingdom, he made a desperate attempt to diminish the effectiveness of the Church, by installing a system of control and government that depended upon a class of professionals called clergy. God's form of rule was no longer active in His Church. The world's system of hierarchical rule was instituted by Satan, the enemy of God, among God's people, however innocent, unsuspecting, or committed the clergy and the people. As a result, most ministers suffer burnout. Many pastors are tempted to give up the ministry, but feel they would be failing God if they did. They have little of the rest Jesus promised would be theirs if they bore His yoke (Matthew 11:28).

Of course, people are being helped. God is using their lives to touch people. The gifts and call of God are without repentance(Romans 11:29). Ministers are known and looked up to by many people. They are appreciated, and rightly so. In many ways, they are fulfilled because of the help they have been to people. Unfortunately, many who gave their whole lives to ministry are going to find Jesus did not even know them.

> Not every one that saith unto me, Lord, Lord, shall enter into the kingdom of heaven; but he that doeth the will of my Father which is in heaven. Many will say to me in that day, Lord, Lord, have we not prophesied in thy name? and in thy name have cast out devils? and in thy name done many wonderful works?
> And then will I profess unto them, I never knew you: depart from me, ye that work iniquity. (Matthew 7:21-23)

As women called into ministry, do we want that rejection after years of labor down here? I think not. My admonition for women who have been called into ministry by God is for them to go to God and get the blueprint He has for them. I am convinced the current pattern of ministry does not work as God intended. I have met many broken, hurting women who have been in the system for years and have not yet been healed. I have seen the pain on their faces. I have seen the tears flow when opportunity is given for them to take off their masks.

A friend of mine told me about the night she spoke at one of the largest churches in this country. She spoke on the hurting woman. An altar call was given after she spoke, and the tremendous response of the women to the altar call amazed everyone. The pastor of the church could not believe the number of hurting women in his church.

Some pastors may not be surprised at that because so many hurting women have come to them for counsel. The needs of hurting people would be met if the people of God operated among each other as God planned it. If everyone was giving and receiving body life, man-made programs would not be needed. In the meantime, counseling ministries are set up to try to meet the needs of the hurting. Some ministers have no idea of the frequency or the extent of the pain and brokenness among their parishioners, even among those who have taken every training course that has come to town.

I have seen enough. I have not seen it all—but I know enough. We need a whole new way of doing things. I could relay story after story from friends and acquaintances who have confided in me over the years. Suffice it to say, broken hearts are not being healed in our current religious structure.

The Unhealed Broken-Hearted Woman

Maybe you still see how good we look on the outside
You don't know the bucket of tears we've just cried
As we were on the road coming to your meeting
You'll never know how close some of us were to suicide.
How could you know that abuse and rejection is getting the best?
When you ask how we are, we always say, "Blessed."
You only see our new dress—and we look so fine!
The smiles, the painted mask, cover the hurt and our distress.

Need for a new model

I strongly believe that it is time for women to stop trying to find a place of ministry in the structures as they exist. We should stay as far away as possible from a system that does not bind up the broken and that allows God's people to become meat to the beasts of the field. I feel so strongly about this because God feels so strongly about it. Listen to His words:

> Thus saith the Lord GOD unto the shepherds; Woe be to the shepherds of Israel that do feed themselves! Should not the shepherds feed the flocks? Ye eat the fat, and ye clothe you with the wool, ye kill them that are fed: but ye feed not the flock. The diseased have ye not strengthened, neither have ye healed that which was sick, neither have ye bound up that which was broken, neither have ye brought again that which was driven away, neither have ye sought that which was lost; but with force and with cruelty have ye ruled them. And they were scattered, because there is no shepherd: and they became meat to all the beasts of the field, when they were scattered. (Ezekiel 34:2-5)

Most people need models. Most people in ministry are following what has been modeled to them over the centuries. The world system's emphasis on buildings, power, control, positions, wealth, lack of accountability, and lording over others is too strongly entrenched in American churches. (And we have exported this to other countries.) I do not believe admonitions are going to cut through it all. In fact, my goal is not to change that system. That's something only God can do. I believe He will take it down and has already begun to do so.

My objective is not to have people disrespect or despise ministers, abandon churches, or even try to convince others to make changes. First, my goal is to wake us up to the need of a prayer covering for all ministers. Although there are some wolves, I believe the majority of ministers are men and women who love God, and are called of God to ministry. I believe God has used them in the lives of many people. I believe God is big enough to work in spite of a system that is less than ideal. God also sometimes winks at things (Acts 17:30). Thank God for His mercy on our traditions and ignorance. We can ask God to forgive us for this ignorance. We can ask God to help us see the need to change. As the passage below indicates, there is a time when we need to repent (change).

> For as I passed by, and beheld your devotions, I found an altar with this inscription, TO THE UNKNOWN GOD. Whom therefore ye ignorantly worship, him declare I unto you. God that made the world and all things therein, seeing that he is Lord of heaven and earth, dwelleth not in temples made with hands; Neither is worshipped with men's hands, as though he needed any thing, seeing he giveth to all life, and breath, and all things; And hath made of one blood all nations of men for to dwell on all the face of the earth, and hath determined the times before appointed, and the bounds of their habitation; That they should seek the Lord, if haply they might feel after him, and find him,

though he be not far from every one of us: For in him we live, and move, and have our being; as certain also of your own poets have said, For we are also his offspring. Forasmuch then as we are the offspring of God, we ought not to think that the Godhead is like unto gold, or silver, or stone, graven by art and man's device. And the times of this ignorance God winked at; but now commandeth all men every where to repent. (Acts 17:22-30)

I personally believe now is the time for a change. My second goal is to see the Body of Christ revived. I want to ask you to pray much for an outpouring of God's Spirit in revival. God can move in a powerful revival, taking up His rightful residence in His temple, the people of God. You can have God's touches, blessings, and even His visits without His indwelling. It will be God's indwelling presence that will present the church without spot or wrinkle (Ephesians 5:27). New wineskins will be needed to hold God's presence. A new form without the presence of God will not change anything. When God pours out His Spirit in revival, He will bring about the changes that are necessary. But we can ask for revival and submit our forms to God for change as needed.

"And no man putteth new wine into old bottles: else the new wine doth burst the bottles, and the wine is spilled, and the bottles will be marred: but new wine must be put into new bottles." (Mark 2:22)

If God has been merciful and patient all these years, certainly you and I can do no less. God tolerated a lot from His people Israel, yet still loved them. Yes, we've been hoodwinked by God's enemy. But God is greater! In the end, God wins. Let's make sure we're fully on His side and under His pattern. Let's do what He says will indicate faith when He returns (Luke 18:8). Let's seriously pray that God will do whatever it takes to take His Church to new heights!

The task for women in ministry

The task before us as women in ministry is to stay on our knees in communion with God, steeping ourselves in His strategies for reclaiming back our families, churches, and cities for the Godly Kingdom. Of necessity, we must empower those whom we serve to do the work of the ministry. We cannot in any way, shape, or fashion be the all-in-all in people's lives. We have to point others to the true source of strength and as He increases in the lives of others, we must decrease.

I do urge all those who have been called into ministry to fall on the Rock before the rock falls on them. We fall on the Rock, Jesus Christ, by letting Him judge the motives of our hearts and allowing Him to meet our need for esteem. The ministry is not the place to have our need for esteem met. True ministry is service. We have to come away from competition, striving for positions, promoting *our* ministries, trying to get noticed, and the like. There is plenty of work to be done for those who are not caught up in the system.

Millions of brokenhearted people are in the church, many of them women. Where are the servants of the Good Shepherd who will bind up the broken and search for the scattered? The current system does not readily allow for healing. Women, there is a place for you: it's at the Master's side. He will tell you His plan for revival. You may or may not be known by thousands. Does that matter? You may live out all your days ministering to one brokenhearted woman who has been so abused that she needs intense, individualized care to heal her heart. But Jesus will know you, because you did His will under His system.

Women called to ministry who want to bring about real change have to leave behind the godless hierarchies of position and power. We have to relegate our desire to be seen and esteemed by people beneath our desire to be known and esteemed by God. We have to be willing to be true servants, serving the Body from below, not ruling from above. Even as our dignity and worth as servants in God's kingdom comes more into focus, we must live out true humility—which only comes by the grace of God, not by exalting ourselves.

What to do now?

We are still in the thick of this current structure. God has not told me to leave it, but has told me to not be *of* it. I need body life ministry to survive spiritually. I find that does not necessarily take place with the current pattern. I applaud the many churches who are moving more to making small group ministry the core of the church ministry. I have attended such a church, but when the Lord has me in places where this is not the case, I get it in other places—usually with the people I know in the church I attend, but at times with other Christians. The times when I neglect body life are times of real spiritual dryness.

Again, I am not calling for a mass exodus from churches. History shows us that any time people depart from their brothers and sisters to start their own "perfect" church or denomination, within one generation it is no less a prison than the church or denomination left behind. The new church or denomination just has a different doctrinal emphasis or different set of practices. So, let's not run away and start our own. God still uses, touches, blesses, visits, teaches, and speaks to us within the current system and in spite of the system. We need the people in the system, and they need us. Besides, the current system is a great place to develop a ministry of prayer.

It is possible to be in the system and not of the system without being disrespectful or rebellious to those in authority. That's only possible by Spirit living. And if the time comes when we clearly have to obey God rather than man, we'll be ready to do that and suffer the consequences because we have learned to be in close communion with God.

Where do we serve?

The opportunities for women to serve abound. The place of ministry ranges from our living room to the corner café to women's conferences and retreats. We don't need an audience of hundreds; six or twelve is fine if that is God's purpose. Serving one person at a time was good enough for Jesus, and it should be good enough for us (John 4:7). If He chooses to use us to speak to the thousands on the hillside, we can do that too. And we can do all this without owning a special building called a "church."

Women, whether you have been called to equip others or to minister life to those God brings into your path, you have been called to be a minister, a servant of the Most High. He will use you now to recover what the enemy has done. God can use you to feed others, to seek the lost, and heal the broken. You can be used of God to fulfill His promise in Ezekiel:

I will feed them in a good pasture, and upon the high mountains of Israel shall their fold be: there shall they lie in a good fold, and in a fat pasture shall they feed upon the mountains of Israel. I will feed my flock, and I will cause them to lie down, saith the Lord GOD. I will seek that which was lost, and bring again that which was driven away, and will bind up that which was broken, and will strengthen that which was sick. (Ezekiel 34:14-16)

The role of small groups

One last thing: as a woman in equipping ministry, be sure you get body life from others. Some of the best body life God may have to give you will probably come from someone you had a role in equipping. Be sure you facilitate body life in any ministry you are involved with.

Body life ministry is best facilitated in small groups. Learn as much as you can about small group ministries which allow all group members to participate. There are a lot of resources out there. Some of the books listed in the bibliography will be helpful.

One excellent book that talks about small group ministry, even in a large church setting, *Faithful Over a Few Things,* was written by George O. McCalep Jr., pastor of Greenforest Baptist Church in Decatur, Georgia. In it, he says a few things about the importance of small groups, defines what a small group is and what it is not, and states the goals of small groups:

> . . . church leaders who have a sincere desire to see their churches grow to the full potential will arrange and/or rearrange and redirect or further direct their time and energy to become faithful in creating small group ministries. This is based on the simple premise that the worship service itself, standing absolutely alone cannot fulfill all of the biblical functions of the church. . . . There will be a plateau that a growing church will reach where the basic fellowship (the *koinonia*) begins to diminish. A word of caution about undermining fellowship. Often we

do not elevate fellowship to its level of importance because we think of it as embracing, handshaking, greeting each other with holy kisses and the like. We think we can accomplish this with an excited five minute intrusion into the worship service. We can do this and still remain strangers in the pews. What a tragedy, brothers and sisters in Christ and strangers in the pews. . . . *Koinonia* means sharing and caring in a demonstrative way. It is derived from *Koinonos* which means partner, companion, partaker, sharer, road buddy.

. . .Small groups are not Sunday School classes, although a Sunday School class may be a small group. Sounds confusing? Not really. The definition is tied to the goal. The goal of a small group is to become biblical in an interpersonal relationship (i.e. loving one another, which will express itself in bearing one another's burden, edifying one another, praying for one another, rejoicing with one another, comforting one another, etc.) As a rule, Sunday School classes and discipleship groups are limited in focus and time relative to fulfilling the essential goal of small group ministry.[3]

There is a need to recover the original blueprint for the people of God. We'll find it as we move on up in the Spirit. I think I have given you enough information in this chapter. I hope I have encouraged you to question what we now have, and to seek God's guidance for something else. Yes, we need to move on up beyond religion to Spirit living if we want to take back what the enemy has stolen from us all these years. This is the goal for everyone in the Body of Christ, but it is of primary importance for women who are called to demonstrate Spirit living in serving others.

As women learn to rely on the power of the Spirit instead of the power of religion to serve others, we may be given the opportunity to demonstrate a new model of Spirit-life ministry. Maybe God will raise up a company of Deborahs and bring the generals to them to find out how to win the battles of our day. Maybe we can be part of that company if we do it the Spirit way—with humility. Perhaps the men and women called to serve the Body of Christ together can find out from God how to recover the original purpose for the Bride of Christ. Let the Bride put on her combat boots, armed to storm the gates of hell.

Prayer:

Father, I want to be used of you any way you want to use me. Remove from me all ideas of how I would like to be used. Please cleanse me from the understanding of ministry that Churchianity has given me. Are there things more important for me than all the committees, programs, and activities I have been so involved in? Teach me anew what it means to minister to you. Let me be a pioneer in the move of Your church beyond religion to Spirit living.

CHAPTER 20

Let's Keep Movin'

"Let us leave the elementary teachings about Christ and go on to maturity."

Hebrews 6:1

THERE IS NOTHING GOD CANNOT do. God can indeed bring new life into our hearts, our families, our churches, and our communities. He is able to do exceedingly more than we can ask or think (Ephesians 3:20). That's why I am not discouraged by the state of the Church as it is. In one day, God is able to change everything and make all things new (Zachariah 3:9).

It is time for a revival. It will be done by God's Holy Spirit, with the cooperation of God's people. This book has explored how we move from religion to relationship building with God and others in the Body by His Spirit. We have not exhausted all that involves. But we trust that we have given you enough to begin.

God is the fountain of all wisdom. He is able to give us wisdom the enemy cannot gainsay or resist (Luke 21:15). He is able to give us strategies that will take our families, churches, communities, and cities back from the hands of the enemy. There was no battle the people of Israel engaged in that they did not win when they sought God's wisdom and followed it. The only times they were defeated were when they did not seek or obey God.

As we conclude, I would like to leave you with a few exhortations and warnings. While I am still learning, and have not arrived, I *am* on my way. Come join me!

Remember, God is in control of your spiritual growth. We cannot grow ourselves up. We only have to cooperate with God as He brings us into the Spirit through the experiences He decides are right for us.

When God uses many trying experiences to grow you up, don't think you are crazy when it seems as if you will explode. Remember, your heart is already broken. God is just putting the pieces together again. None of the king's horses and none of the king's men could do it, but King Jesus can mend our broken hearts (Luke 4:18).

Remember, the trials are worth it. Hang in there. The more you go through, the better equipped you will be to destroy the enemy's works. I don't know about you, but I want to be able to do some serious damage to Satan's kingdom.

Growing up spiritually is not as complicated as Christian religion would make it. The best advice comes in the simple words of an old song: "Trust and Obey." There is no other way to grow in Jesus. We have to believe, and trust God to complete His work in us. We have to do what He tells us to do. Just do it! Whatever it is that you know to do, do it.

Pursue the things of the Spirit. Don't be so afraid of making mistakes that you go nowhere. If you make a mistake, God will correct you. Be willing to turn to others in the family of God in your learning process. In the multitude of counselors, there is safety (Proverbs 11:14).

We've talked mostly about the Holy Spirit. The Holy Spirit is one member of the Godhead. He has been sent by the Father to work in our lives. But remember His purpose is to glorify Christ (John 16:13-14). The Holy Spirit is the agent; Christlikeness is the result.

The foundation of the Word

The most important thing I can say about the things of the Spirit is: do not neglect the Word of God. The Word of God is foundational to all God wants to do in our lives. The Word tells us how to pray. The Word heals our broken hearts. It instructs us in righteousness. It is profitable for doctrine, correction and reproof

(2 Timothy 3:16). The Word will keep us from sin (Psalm 119:11). The Word shows how the Spirit of God leads us. Without the Word, we more than likely will be led away by deceiving spirits, doctrines of demons, and traditions of men. Doctrines of demons and counterfeit spiritual experiences will always take us away from simplicity in Christ (2 Corinthians 11:3).

All doctrines originating from demons have a biblical base. It becomes a doctrine of demons when anything other than Christ is the focal point. We cannot let anything keep us from pursuing Jesus Christ as Lord of all!

Pursuing Jesus fully means dying to our selfish, carnal ways. It requires sacrifice, even a willingness to lay our promises on the altar in order to fully receive the provision of God (Genesis 22:1-14). He alone is enough!

Many of God's people who have started out pursuing Jesus have come across a table with a large variety of beautifully wrapped packages. All of these have tons of scriptural references written on them. Among many others, we find packages of joy, peace, healing, prosperity, fruitfulness, love—all good things promised to us by God. Too often what happens is we get all caught up in the packages and forget to continue pursuing Jesus. All of these promises are yes and amen in Christ (2 Corinthians 1:20). Satan tricks us into pursuing the promises apart from Christ.

Anchored in the Word

In order to be women of the Spirit, we have to be anchored in the God's Word. We cannot be anchored in spiritual experiences, no matter how powerful they may be. Only the Word will keep us on the right path. To be anchored in the Word, we must be doers of the Word, and not hearers only (James 1:22).

Many of us know the Word, but when it comes down to doing the things the Word says to do—such as esteeming others better than ourselves; not always looking out for our own interests, but for the needs of others; speaking well of those who speak evil of us; doing kind deeds to those who do us wrong, and praying for those who despitefully use us or persecute us—we don't have that great a track record.

It would be a serious mistake to think we can pursue things of the Spirit and not be obedient to the Word of God. The Word and the Spirit go hand in hand. An overemphasis on the Word without a corresponding emphasis on the Spirit could lead to legalism, while an overemphasis on the things of the Spirit without a corresponding emphasis on the Word could lead to pride and deception.

The world has enough people to preach sermons. What the world needs now is to see a few sermons walking about. That, my friends, is our destiny. Let us not take the easy way out, for as we all know, it is easier to talk the walk than to walk the talk. Let's do what we need to do to get healed from our own brokenness. Healing came for me as I opened myself up to transparent relationships with members of the Body of Christ. Others may get the same kind of healing in a formal counseling setting. I took training in the Exchange Life counseling modality to equip me to help others. It was helpful to me as well. I highly recommend this method of Biblical counseling because it recognizes the necessity of dying to self in the midst of our problems.

Let's move on up and help bring others on up. Many of us need to invest our lives into a few people's lives; we need to teach others what we have learned (Hebrews 5:12). Let's go on to maturity (Hebrews 6:1).There is plenty to do as we ourselves are getting healed. Perhaps you know broken hearted women who are spiritually immature, but who sincerely desire to walk with God. They are not going to make it without some help. God has placed you in their lives for a purpose. Begin by praying for them. I have found a real help in my prayer life with the prayers Paul prayed. They are found in Colossians 1:9-11; Philippians 1:9-11; Ephesians 1:16-20; 3:14-19; 1Thessalonians 3:9-13; 5:23; 2 Thessalonians 1:11-12. I pray these prayers for people God has placed in my life. God will lead you to what else you are to do. That's what so exciting about God. He'll talk with us on a daily basis if we're willing to listen!

The Kingdom want ads

Our communities are in dire need of watchwomen, porters, and gap standers. Gap standers stand in the gap when there are holes in the walls or hedges surrounding our families, churches, and communities. By standing in the gap, they prevent the enemy from going in and out to steal, kill, and destroy.

Watchwomen go up in the Spirit, stand on the wall, and look out to see what the enemy is trying to do. They communicate to the porters, who guard the door. The porters shut the gates and the enemy is unable to bring his mess into our communities.

I believe that in times past, say fifty or more years ago, our mothers and grandmothers were the watchwomen, porters, and gap standers. They may not even have known what to call their roles, but by the Spirit, they did what needed to be done. The Devil may have tried to bring crack into the community fifty years ago, but he couldn't succeed. In order to be able to accomplish what he is doing today, he had to push women out of these vitally important positions.

We need women who are willing to go back to the walls, gates, and hedges and bring change. This will only be possible if women return to Spirit living. It can be done. It will be done. That's what this book is all about. God wants women to move on up to another place in Him so that, as partners with Him, we can bring our families, communities, churches, and cities out of the clutches of Satan. God has sent me as a recruiting officer.

I am a servant of God, and as His servant I believe that He has called me to come along beside ministers to help them in their job of building up the saints so that we can all do the work of the ministry (Ephesians 4:12). More than anything else, I desire to see the Body of Christ be the Church against whom the gates of hell will not prevail.

May God continue to raise up women who live in the Spirit. May God fulfill in us the destiny for which we were created. As a result, may the men in our lives once again see the beauty of God manifested in us and be drawn to the things of the Spirit.

We must call upon God to help us live by His Word and His Spirit. God wants to raise up women who, by living out the Word, have brought their flesh under subjection to the Holy Spirit. I'm going to move on up! Are you?

Moving On Up

You'll have to learn to live in the Spirit, you can't just visit
You'll need the knowledge of the Word and the power of the Spirit
Don't turn back, just keep pressing on through to that place of rest
Lean on Him, when you don't understand, He really does know best
You'll go from a baby, through childhood, adolescence to maturity
When all your props are removed and He becomes your only security
To move on up under the shadow of His wings, to that secret place
Let go of religion, because it won't be by works; only by His grace

End Notes

Chapter One

1. Rebecca Osaigbovo, *Chosen Vessels: Women of Color, Keys to Change*. (Detroit:Dabar Publishing, 1992), p. 54.

Chapter Two

1. Victoria Johnson, *Restoring Broken Vessels: Confronting the At tack on Female Sexuality*. (Detroit: Dabar Publishing, 1995), p. 16.

Chapter Three

1. Mary Jean Pidgeon, J.C. Webster, *We've Come a Long Way, Baby! So Where Do We Go From Here*. (Tulsa: Harrison House, 1994), pp. 57, 58.
2. Ibid., pp. 60, 61.
3. Kunjufu Jawanza. *Adam! Where Are You? Why Most Black Men Don't Go to Church*. (Chicago: African American Images, 1994), p.73

Chapter Four

1. Rick Joyner. *There Were Two Trees In The Garden*. (Charlotte: Morningstar Publications, 1986). p. 1.
2. Craig Nakken. *The Addictive Personality: Understanding Compul sion in Our Lives*. (San Francisco: Harper & Row Publishing, 1988), p. 4.

Chapter Seven

1. David Alsobrook. *Keep Yourself From Idols*. (Paducah, Ken tucky: David Alsobrook Ministries, 1986), p. 67.
2. Os Guinness and John Seel. *No God But God: Breaking With the Idols of Our Age*. (Chicago: Moody Press, 1992) p. 16.
3. Judson Cornwall. *Things We Adore: How to Recognize and Get Free of Idolatry*. (Shippensburg, PA: Destiny Image Publishers, 1991), p. 18.
4. Craig Nakken. *The Addictive Personality*, p. 10.

5. Cornwall, *Things We Adore,* p. 70.

6. Guiness and Seel, *No God But God,* p. 53.

Chapter Eight

1. Les Carter and FrankMinirth. *The Anger Workbook.* (Nash ville:Thomas Nelson Publishers, 1993), p. 8.

2. Dwight Carlson, *Overcoming Hurts and Anger.* (Eugene, Ore gon: Harvest House Publishers, 1981), p. 50.

Chapter Fifteen

1. Richard W. Dortch. *Fatal Conceit.* (Green Forest, Arizona: New Leaf Press, 1993), p. 27.

2. Edwards, Gene. *Climb The Highest Mountain.* (Beaumont, Texas: The SeedSowers, 1984), pp. 84, 85.

3. Watchman Nee. *Love Not The World.* (Fort Washington, PA: Christian Literature Crusade, 1968), pp. 13, 14.

4. Ibid., pp. 21, 22.

Chapter Sixteen

1. Gayle D. Erwin. *The Jesus Style.* (Waco, Texas: Word Books, 1988), p. 5.

2. Charles R. Swindoll. *Improving Your Serve: The Art of Unselfish Living.* (Waco, Texas: Word Books, 1981), p. 21.

3. Erwin, *The Jesus Style* pp. 55, 56.

4. Ibid., p. 59.

Chapter Nineteen

1. Peter C. Wagner. *Prayer Shield.* (Ventura, California: Regal Books, 1992), p. 79.

2. James Rutz, *The Open Church.* (Auburn, Maine: SeedSow ers, 1992), pp. 44-47.

2. George O. McCalep, Jr. *Faithful Over a Few Things: Seven Criti cal Church Growth Principles.* (Lithonia, GA: Orman Press, 1996), pp. 101, 102.

Bibliography

Beckham, William A. *The Second Reformation: Reshaping the Church for the Twenty-First Century.* Houston: Touch Publications.

Bright, Bill. *The Coming Revival.* Orlando: NewLife Publica tions, 1995.

Dollar, Creflo A. Dollar, Jr. *Exposing The Spirit of Competitive Jeal ousy.* Edmond, OK: Vision Communications, 1993.

Edwards, Gene. *The Highest Life.* Wheaton: Tyndale House Publishers, Inc., 1989.

Hagin, Kenneth E. *Growing Up, Spiritually.* Tulsa: Kenneth Hagin Ministries, 1976.

Jacobsen, Wayne. *The Naked Church.* Eugene, Oregon: Harvest House Publishers, 1987.

Massey, James Earl. *Spiritual Discipline: Growth Through the Prac tice of Prayer, Fasting, Dialogue, & Worship.* Grand Rapids: Francis Asbury Press, 1985.

Meyer, Joyce. *If Not For the Grace of God.* Tulsa: Harrison House, 1995.

Murray, Andrew. *The Spirit of Christ.* Fort Washington, Pennsylva nia: Christian Literature Crusade, 1963.

Nee, Watchman. *The Release of the Spirit.* Indianapolis: Sure Foundation, 1965.

Nee, Watchman. *The Spiritual Man.* New York: Christian Fellow ship Publisher, Inc., 1968.

Ness, Alex, W. *Triumphant Christian Living.* Downsview, On tario, Canada: Agape Publications

Neighbour, Ralph W., Jr. *Where Do We Go From Here? A Guide book for the Cell Group Church.* Houston: Touch Publica tions, 1990.

Potter, Jerold C. *Your Mouth Can Be As Deadly As A Pistol.* Los Angeles: Word Of Faith And Power Prison Ministry, 1989.

Prince, Derek. *Does Your Tongue Need Healing?* Springdale, PA: Whitaker House, 1986.

Shankle, Randy. *The Merismos.* Tulsa: Christian Pub lishing Services, 1987.

Sherrer, Quin & Garlock, Ruthanna. *A Woman's Guide to Spirit-Filled Living.* Ann Arbor: Servant Publications, 1996.

Snyder, Graydon F. *Ante Pacem: Archaeological Evidence of Church Life Before Constantine.* Mercer University Press, The SeedSow ers, 1985.

Snyder, Howard A. *Radical Renewal: The Problem of Wineskins To day.* Houston: Touch Publications, 1996.

Stedman, Ray C. *Body Life.* Glendale, California: Regal Books Division, G/L Publications, 1972.

Trulin, Pastor Paul G. *The Making Of A Christian.* Sacramento: Trinity Life Press, 1978.

Walker, Clarence. *Breaking Strong Holds in the African American Family.* Grand Rapids: Zondervan Publishing, 1996.

Wallis, Arthur. *China Miracle: A Silent Explosion.* Columbia, Mis souri: Cityhill Publishing, 1986.

Warren, Neil Clark. *Make Anger Your Ally.* Colorado Springs: Fo cus On The Family Publishing, 1990.

*Inclusion of any author's book does not constitute recommenda-tion of the totality of the author's teachings.

Other Books and Resources

Restoring Broken Vessels by Victoria Johnson is a book that breaks the sexual yoke of Satan against women. The writer shares, through personal experiences and research, clear instruc-tions for help, healing and freedom from guilt.

Using Biblical principles, practical illustrarions and thought provoking questions, *Chosen Vessels* examines the spiritual past, present and God-ordained future of African American women.

"Becoming a House" of Prayer is a "Chosen Vessels" seminar offered by Rebecca Osaigbovo. It teaches the prayers that are necessary for healing according to 2 Chronicles 7:14. This seminar is done in churches or as a program for retreats. It is scheduled at different places around the country at invitation and 2 to 3 times in the Metro-Detroit area.

"Standing in the Gap" is a second seminar offered by Rebecca Osaigbovo. While the focus of "Becoming a House of Prayer" is the prayers that will bring individual change, "Standing in the Gap" concentrates on the prayers that will bring change to our families, communities, and nation.

Audio and/ Video Tape Series, including Bible Study Notes:
"Becoming a House of Prayer"
Other titles available.

To order with credit cards:
For distributor information:
Other order information:
Detroit seminar information:

1/800-233-0086

For all other inquires or to obtain information on having Rebecca minister in your community, please contact:

Dabar Publishing Company
P.O. box 35377
Detroit, MI 48235
Phone: 313/531-7534
Fax: 313/531-7660